CONTENTS

Title Page	2
Disclaimer	4
INTRODUCTION	6
HOW TO USE THIS BOOK	19
Part One	20
Chapter One	22
Chapter Two	33
Chapter Three	48
Part Two	55
Chapter Four	57
Chapter Five	70
Part Three	82
Chapter Six	84
Chapter Seven	92
Chapter Eight	104
Part Four	122
Chapter Nine	124
Chapter Ten	140

Part Five	151
Chapter Eleven	153
Chapter Twelve	166
CONCLUSION	177
About the Author	179
Bibliography	181

TAPPING INTO ABUNDANCE

*Using EFT and Law of Attraction
to Change Your Mindset and
Turn Your Life Around*

Sandra Inman

DISCLAIMER

This book has been written to provide information to help you remove your blocks to achieving your goals. Every effort has been made to make this information as complete and accurate as possible. However, there may be mistakes in typography or content.

This Publication is distributed with the understanding that the author is not engaged in rendering professional psychotherapy, psychiatric, health, medical, career or financial advice or services of any kind.

All questions relevant to the specific professional psychological, psychiatric, health, medical, career and financial needs of the reader should be addressed to practicing members of those professions.

Any person experiencing financial, career concerns, anxiety, depression, stress, health, or relationship issues, should consult with a qualified professional in those areas before commencing any new financial plan or transaction, career strategy, change in personal relationships, exercise program, or following any of the teachings, methods, and suggestions described in this book. This book is not a substitute for the reader enlisting qualified professionals to assist with the reader's specific circumstances, issues, and problems.

The purpose of this book is to educate. The author does

not warrant that the information contained in this book is fully complete and shall not be responsible for any errors or omissions.

The author shall have neither liability nor responsibility to any person or entity with respect to any loss or damage caused or alleged to be caused directly or indirectly by this book. The book and the contents herein are provided without any warranty, express or implied, as to their effect, completeness, or results received.

Copyright © 2020 – Sandra Inman.

All rights are reserved. No part of this book may be reproduced or transmitted in any form without the written permission of the author.

INTRODUCTION

Would you like to feel more in control of your life?

Do you want to feel financially secure knowing that all of your expenses can easily be taken care of?

Wouldn't it be wonderful to have that awesome relationship you've always wanted or to rekindle that romance with your current partner?

How amazing would it be to fully live the life you want to live with joy, peace and an empowered sense of self!

Whether it's the career, relationship or financial security that you've always wanted, developing your ability to attract to you what you want can certainly make your life easier and happier.

This creative power is known by many names. You've probably come across terms such as: manifestation, law of attraction, magic and magnetism.

What do they really mean?

Do they even work?

Are there really people out there who can and do successfully create the life they want to live?

Let's talk a little about the law of attraction.

The term Law of attraction is simply a modern name for a very old practice.

Most cultures past and present have a history of practising magic. Yes, I said Magic!

Magic is simply another term for manifestation and law of attraction.

Before the law of attraction become the popular new age term for magic, people were practicing manifestation in a variety of ways. Many cultures practised magic, however, in western culture it was considered unacceptable for a very long time.

Magic was believed to be something evil, dark and taboo. Yet, magic and law of attraction use the same principles and are essentially the same thing.

Both magic and law of attraction allow people to create the life they want to live through the power of thought, emotion, intention and focus.

And you have access to this creative power too!

In many ways, the law of attraction is bringing the magic back into people's lives.

I've been practising magic for 30 years as a Wiccan and it is far from being evil or dark. Magic is simply neutral lifeforce energy. It's neither good nor evil.

Neuroscientists are learning so much about how our brains work. Scientists studying quantum physics are revealing very interesting discoveries about how the universe works. What we thought was "hocus pocus" is now beginning to find its way into many people's everyday lives.

The law of attraction is based on the premise that what we think about the most we create in reality. If we are able to control our thinking then we should be able to exercise a large degree of control over our own lives.

Magic challenges the belief that we are like the jellyfish being swept around in the ocean tides with no control over where we go. Instead, it dares us to take responsibility for ourselves, our thinking and our lives.

Being able to control our own destiny sounds very appealing and many people are successful at doing it. However, it's not just a matter of thinking about what you want and having it. It's more complex than that.

I've spent the last 30 years being involved in communities where magic is a part of life. Yet, I still didn't really understand how it all worked until I was introduced to the law of attraction.

I always had an interest in psychology and how the mind works but never connected that to manifestation until I underwent hypnotherapy and started studying Emotional Freedom Technique.

Once I started seeing the connections, I began to have a better understanding about what was happening in my own life and how I could make my magic work better for me.

I also wanted to help other people within my community to do the same. So, I became qualified as a hypnotherapist and Emotional Freedom Technique coach.

I am passionately determined to help others realise that they can manifest happier lives with more joy and abundance. This certainly beats living a life full of stress and the struggles of day to day survival.

You see, it's not just a case of knowing about the law of attraction. You need to really understand how it all works in order to make it work better. There are so many myths out there about manifestation that it's easy to think it's all just rubbish or that it's just too hard.

Over the years, I have used the law of attraction to organise my life the way I want it. For example, I always wanted to live by the sea. Through using a simple technique that I'll show you later in the book, I managed to do just that. Now, I can enjoy the beach as often as I want.

I've used magic to attract jobs, relationships, opportunities and situations into my life.

I'll be honest though, it hasn't always worked out the way I wanted it to and in this book I'll share with you the reasons why.

Now, I also want to mention that the law of attraction can be used for anything you want. It can be used every day. It doesn't have to be only for the big things; it can be as simple as finding a car park in a busy shopping complex.

I've used a number of different techniques and methods over the years but they all share the same basic components which I'll be sharing with you throughout this book.

The most important thing I've found is that your subconscious mind must be in alignment with your conscious intention, otherwise it just won't work out the way you want.

One of the most common complaints I hear from people is, "Why can't I make the law of attraction (or magic) work for me?" In truth, it is working for them. It always works regardless of how conscious we are of the fact.

We are magnetic beings and we are constantly attracting people and resources to us all day long. What we should be asking is why it isn't working for us when we are **DELIBERATELY** trying to attract something we want into our lives.

There is a lot of good advice out there regarding manifestation and law of attraction. If you're familiar with law of attraction you're probably already doing the vision boards, visualising your bigger and better future and doing all of the affirmations. That's great! Keep it up! If these motivate you, then keep them in your tool kit. But are they enough?

The problem that many people have when it comes to law of attraction is that they can't get it to work for them the way they want it to.

Are you having trouble manifesting what you want into your life?

Are you having trouble believing that you can have all of the wonderful things in life that you want?

If you've answered, yes, to these questions then you've no doubt got some limiting beliefs blocking you. And you may be surprised to know that some of those beliefs are so deep within your subconscious mind that you don't even know they're there.

The major reason for this is that you have been conditioned into believing very limiting impressions about yourself and the things that you desire. This brain washing has occurred throughout your life and it limits your ability to magnetically attract the people and experiences that you want to you.

Our life experiences can condition us to perceive the world in a very limited way. As we listen to parents, teachers, society and our peers, we take in messages of scarcity, lack and doubt about our own abilities and capacity for success.

What we experience and learn from others encourages us to form certain beliefs about life and the world around us. Many of these beliefs are about lack, self-doubt, unworthiness and fear. These limiting beliefs prevent us from reaching our full potential.

Perhaps you've tried to change your own limiting beliefs in order to manifest the life you want. However, there are very few tools out there that can really transform those limiting beliefs into helpful ones that support your goals.

Our beliefs are so programmed into us that they can be very difficult to release and change. Of course, we can use affirmations, but if the beliefs are so deeply embedded in our subconscious mind, then we're going to need a stronger and more powerful tool to clear those beliefs and supercharge those new affirmations.

What the Tapping into Abundance program aims to do is teach you a technique that you can easily do for yourself anywhere, at any time, that addresses those negative beliefs, releases them, and then reprograms your mind with new positive and powerful beliefs.

Is that ok with you?

I will also show you some potent techniques that you can use to increase your magnetic energy and attract what you want to you.

Does that sound good to you?

This method is called Emotional Freedom Technique or Tapping and it's a powerful tool that you have literally at your fingertips. You simply tap your fingers on a number of acupuncture meridian points while focusing on a negative belief or feeling.

It's so easy to do. You can even use this method to powerfully reinforce the positive affirmations once you've cleared those limiting programs.

At the end of this program you will:

Understand your own magnetic ability and how to increase its effectiveness.

Discover your blocks to manifestation and skilfully eliminate them.

Access the power within you that directs the universal energy toward your goals.

Know yourself and what you really want from life.

Fast track your ability to live the life you were born to live.

Essentially, once you work through this program, you'll have the knowledge and skills available to you to help you achieve the love, the career or whatever else you strive for.

Do you like the sound of that?

I'm not making any promises. Significant change takes work. It takes years of work.

Don't expect that this book will solve all of your problems tomorrow or the next day. It's your first step and your guide to greater things but it won't do the work for you.

Program Outline

Magic is an art form. All art forms require skill and you can acquire this skill by following this simple 5 step process.

Step One

You need to know what the law of attraction is and

how your mind and the quantum universe work. Why? Knowledge is power. The more you know, the better you'll be able to find ways to magnetise what you want and remove the blocks to it.

Once you know how things work all you need to do is decide what it is you want to bring into your life. This often goes beyond objects and things. Underneath the desire for shiny new cars and grand houses are deeper yearnings.

Many people tell me that they have an inner knowing that there is more to life than the hustle and bustle of modern life. They feel that they just aren't living life with a deep enough meaning or sense of their purpose.

Our modern lifestyle often distracts us from doing the things we really want to do and being with the people we really want to be with. We are "doing" rather than "living".

Knowing what you really want can be difficult to find because it's often buried under years of conditioning.

Most of us knew instinctively what we wanted to do as small children, but years of 'reality' and social programming have forced these callings to the back of our subconscious mind.

Our belief that they just aren't possible anymore forms a barrier around those callings to such an effect that we have forgotten they were even there. Many of us have become numb to our dreams.

Step Two

Once you know what it is that you want you need to determine how you feel about it. This is when you may discover some uncomfortable feelings.

These feelings need to be explored and if they are not helpful to you then you need to change them. This is a very important part of the process and the one that is usually left out.

Step Three

You must explore your limiting beliefs about yourself and the world around you because they determine how successful you are at attracting what you want to you.

Step Four

This is where you can have fun and start creating what it is that you want using a number of fun and easy techniques to help you focus your intent.

Step Five

Finally, you can sit back and let the universe respond to you. This is so often one of the hardest aspects to manifestation. You must learn to get out of the way of the universe. Don't worry, I'll show you how to do this.

Does all of that sound ok to you?

As an old teacher of mine used to say, "Try it and see, don't try it and see."

The Tapping into Abundance book combines these 5 steps into 5 easy to follow parts.

WARNING:

This is a practical book and you will be doing a number of activities.

The law of attraction is about doing and not just reading and hoping.

It's not about wishful thinking and daydreaming.

It does require commitment and concentrated effort on your part. But don't you think that living the life you really came here to live is worth the effort?

Part One

Part One provides you with the knowledge that you'll need to understand the law of attraction and how your mind works and why it has a prominent place in your ability to magnetically attract the prosperity, relationships and good health that you want to you.

Chapter One

In this section you'll learn about magnetism and how it relates to manifestation and law of attraction. You will gain a clear understanding of the law of attraction which will help you become more successful with it.

Chapter Two

In section two you'll discover the role your mind plays in the law of attraction and how it can sabotage your results.

You'll learn how the brain is a transceiver and how quantum science is challenging what you thought you knew about yourself and the world around you.

Chapter Three

We'll delve into the concept of mental programs and how they influence your life. You'll also do some activities to explore your unique energy signature and how your vibration affects you and your environment.

Part Two

This is where you'll learn the amazing tapping modality called Emotional Freedom Technique and use it to explore what it is that you want to attract and why.

Chapter Four

I'll show you how to tap and give you a little background as to why it works so well. Then you'll be ready to start the 5 step process.

Chapter Five

Time to explore what it is that you really want and why you want it. That 'why' is very important! You'll find the essence of what you desire which will help you magnetise what you want to you.

Part Three

In Part Three you'll thoroughly explore the reasons why you're not getting what you want and why it's been so difficult until now to reach your full potential. We'll also explore how you can change that.

Chapter Six

You will uncover the hidden reasons why you want what you want. You'll learn how to use this knowledge to design your life according to your heart's desire rather than from your head.

Chapter Seven

With the use of tapping, you will become aware of your deeper opposing beliefs and start changing them subconsciously. This is a tough section but it will pay off in the long run.

Chapter Eight

Discover why it's important to focus on the now and how you can tap your way into appreciation of what you have ALREADY achieved.

Part Four

This is where you'll learn the art of magnetic attraction enabling you to be a very powerful magnet to what you want.

Chapter Nine

This is where you will learn to live your new story both imaginatively and in reality, so that you become a more powerful magnet to what you want.

Chapter Ten

This section is important. I will show you how to get out of the common problem of obsessing about results and worrying about how it's all going to happen.

This is one of the major barriers to successful manifestation. You have to learn to get out of the way of the universe and trust its ability to bring you what you want.

Part Five

I'll show you step by step what to do to make yourself more powerful and how to project that power out into the universe. There are a number of fun ways to do this with and without tapping.

Chapter Eleven

In this chapter I will go through the 5-step process and add some fun tools and techniques that you can use to enhance your energy and focus your power.

Chapter Twelve

I will provide you with powerful tips on how you can continue to develop your magical ability and what you can do on a daily basis to keep yourself up to speed with designing your life the way you want it.

I encourage you to try out every activity throughout this book so that you can better understand how it all works together. You won't know just how powerful you can be unless you do it.

Manifestation is both an art and a craft and no one ever became good at their art without actively spending time perfecting their skill. The more you practice manifesting the better you'll get at it.

HOW TO USE THIS BOOK

This book is designed to be a step by step process whereby you will develop your ability to magnetise what you want to you.

In order to fully master the process, I recommend that you work through each part one by one. You can take as much time as you like but I would recommend that you spend no more than 2 weeks on each part.

Personal development and change are like a spiral. We often keep having to come back to where we've been before. Each time we come back though, it's on a different level.

You may find that over time you will come back to various chapters and get something different from them each time you repeat them.

If you are at any time feeling emotionally overwhelmed by what the tapping brings up for you, please seek out help from a qualified therapist or practitioner. This book is not meant to be a replacement for any therapy or medical assistance you may be already considering or undertaking.

PART ONE

YOUR MIND IS LIKE A MAGNET

Let's begin with an activity!

Close your eyes, take some slow deep breaths and think of something that you wanted that you recently received or achieved. Once you've thought of it, open your eyes and answer the following questions.

Can you recall some of the feelings you had before and after you received what you wanted?

Were your thoughts positive?

Did you have an inner knowing that you would get it?

How did you feel once you got it?

Do you remember what you thought after you received it?

You manifest unconsciously all of the time. It's a natural process that happens constantly. Even if you aren't aware of it, you are using your thoughts and feelings to create what you want.

The art of manifestation is a process of magnetically drawing your desires, ideas and dreams from your imagination into your outer reality and the key player in all of this is your mind.

CHAPTER ONE

Magic, Manifestation and Magnetism

What is Law of Attraction?

When the movie, *The Secret,* was released, everyone became excited about having an ability to attract whatever they desired merely by thinking about it a lot.

Thinking about what we want is one of the ingredients to manifesting our goals, but there is more to it than that.

The law of attraction is the name given to the concept that whatever we think about the most, we will receive.

Another way of looking at it is that our intentions are mirrored back to us. It's a give and take relationship between us and the greater universal mind or consciousness.

There is no judgement or punishment. There is just a reflection of what we are focusing on being mirrored back to us.

You could think of the Universe as a collective consciousness and that we are extensions of this mass consciousness. Life is the result of greater consciousness wanting to see and experience itself.

Sound a bit abstract? Well yes, but there really is no other way to explain it. People who follow the law of attraction come from vast religious and non-religious backgrounds, so it's not meant to be limited to a particular spiritual path. In fact, it doesn't actually matter what your beliefs are, it still works.

You don't even need to believe any of this to make it work for you. I'm just giving you a brief run down on the spiritual philosophy behind it.

People all over the world have a history of practising the law of attraction, however, it was never called that.

What these people did was commonly called magic. They used a variety of methods to heal, secure food and basically live life with more ease. They all knew that they could affect change by combining their intention with will and specific actions.

People have referred to these practitioners of the art as shamans, witches, magicians, sorcerers and more recently, magic workers.

The law of attraction is simply a modern term for our ability to be able to attract people, events, situations and things to us so that we can create the life we want to live. Much like the shamans, witches and magicians did and still do.

Even though it has been known by different names from past to present, it's still the same thing.

Looking at it from a quantum physics point of view, our ability to manifest is more about our unified connection to the Universe.

It all occurs between our subconscious mind and the greater universal force in a feedback loop of sorts.

The greater universal consciousness or collective consciousness which we are all a part of can be thought of as God, Goddess, All Mind, All That Is etc. It doesn't actually matter how we relate to it as it will always relate to us, because we are a part of it and it is a part of us.

As I said before, it doesn't matter if you believe this or not. This is just the background of where the current thought is coming from. What's important is that your subconscious mind plays a key role in creating your reality and that's what we're going to be focusing on in this book.

You see we are creating our reality with our subconscious mind all of the time; we just don't know it. We create both the good and the bad in our lives largely with our thoughts.

Even if you're new to the idea of law of attraction you have been using it all of your life. Now it's time to master the art of creating so you can design your life consciously.

The alternative is that things remain the same as they are now. That means the same debt, loneliness, financial insecurity, unrewarding job or whatever it is that you have in your life that you really don't want.

Now that's fine if what you have is all you want and everything is going really well for you. There is no pressure here to change anything about your life if you're happy.

It's important to emphasise that you are creating your life even as you read this, and you can choose to continue as you are or live a life by your conscious design.

Magnetism and Manifestation

Our magnetism is our ability to attract things to us. Our brains and hearts have a strong magnetic force around them. This force has been scientifically measured. Our magnetism is influenced by how we feel and how we feel is the result of what we think.

All atomic structures vibrate. We are made of atoms, so we vibrate too. We have our own vibration and our vibration is influenced by our beliefs and perceptions. I'll talk about the science of this in the next chapter.

When it comes to law of attraction, most people are only aware of what they are consciously wanting. We are told to write down what we want and regularly visualise ourselves having it or cut out pictures of our goals and display them around the house.

There is one downside to this. When you are constantly focusing on your desire you're not living as if the desire has already happened. Every time, you see what you want on your wall you are being reminded that you don't have it yet. This can actually block your ability to attract it.

In this book, I'm going to show you a number of ways that you can use the law of attraction successfully to create what you want. But first we need to align your subconscious mind with your conscious desire.

When your subconscious mind is in alignment with your conscious desire then you can manifest what you want into your life with ease. That's why it's important to know what your beliefs are and change them if they aren't supporting your vision for your future.

Even though the law of attraction is simple, it is also

complex. It's a paradox. You see, in order to make the law of attraction work you need to know deep down inside yourself that it's already worked.

Now that can be harder than it seems. If you have a belief that you can never achieve the lifestyle you want then you're not going to be able to know deep inside yourself that it's going to work.

Instead, all you're going to know is that it isn't possible for you.

I'll show you how this works:

Think about something you want right now that seems unachievable.

Now, what do you feel in your gut? Do you feel like you know you're going to achieve it or does it feel more like something inside you is saying, "don't be ridiculous, you could never have that?"

If you're feeling the latter in this activity then you need to look at your limiting beliefs and change them.

Our vibration isn't only affected by thinking about our goal. It's how we **FEEL** about our goal that provides the energy to propel the thought out into the universal matrix. That's one of the missing ingredients of the "The Secret".

Emotion and Magnetism

You need emotion to give your intention energy. The successful use of the law of attraction relies on us being in a happy and calm mental state where we can maintain a high level of self-control.

We manifest things all of the time, but we're usually not aware of it. This is because our intentions are subconscious as well as conscious.

Unfortunately, we're not very aware of what our subconscious intentions are and that's where most of the problems with manifestation originate.

Our positive thoughts make us feel positive emotions which reinforce our positive thinking. It's a feedback loop. Our negative thoughts do the same but in reverse. The universe doesn't differentiate between positive and negative thoughts and so it will respond in kind.

As I have said before and will keep repeating throughout this book; you manifest anyway regardless of whether you believe in law of attraction or not. All you need to do is decide what kind of life you want and if you are willing to give this a try or not.

Yes, it all comes down to choice. It works even if you don't believe in it because you are doing it anyway, just not consciously.

So, if you haven't already, do that little activity above and really notice how you feel when you think about your desire.

The Mind and the Mirror

There are two major mistakes that people make when trying to manifest something. First, they only use their thoughts to manifest what they want and second, they visualise their desire without giving any attention to what they are feeling about the desire.

If this is what you've been doing up until now, don't worry, it's not your fault. That's how law of attraction has been taught. It goes like this; think of what you want and then visualise it happening.

Unfortunately, that's only half the process.

Our vibration is affected by our emotions and our emotions are affected by our beliefs and perceptions. When we focus on what we don't want then the universe mirrors that back to us by giving us more of the same which is what we don't want.

When we focus on what we want and feel good about it the universe will reflect that back to us and we will get more of the same which is what we do want.

I'm using the analogy of a mirror because it's the easiest one to use. It's not quite like a mirror but more like a feedback loop.

We don't always get exactly what we are consciously projecting out as it often comes back to us differently to what we may have expected. In fact, it usually responds in a way far better than we could ever imagine.

The problem occurs when we think we are focusing on what we want but subconsciously we are focusing on the opposite.

Take John for example.

John tries so hard to positively focus on getting a better paying job but his subconscious mind is programmed to believe that he isn't good enough for a higher paying position or occupation.

So how does this affect John?

Well John moans about the fact that he is stuck where he is. He may say that he doesn't know enough or that other people always do better than he does. He may blame the government and the economy. He may see himself as disadvantaged in some way.

Well, John's subconscious mind is constantly sending

a message to the universe telling it that he isn't good enough, he doesn't know enough, he doesn't deserve it and that he's a loser.

The universe is responding by giving him more evidence of his beliefs because that's what he's telling it he wants subconsciously.

Do the following exercise to get a feel for what I'm talking about here.

Activity 1

Go to a mirror and look at your reflection.

Think about something funny and look at yourself. Observe how you look.

What is being reflected back to you?

Now think of something that makes you angry. Observe how you look.

What is being reflected back to you?

It's like looking at two different people isn't it. When you looked at yourself happy and laughing it probably made you want to laugh more.

How did you feel when you looked at the angry reflection?

Now think of something that you want but don't feel confident about receiving.

Look at yourself in the mirror and say: "I'm going to (name the desire)."

Is the person looking back at you convincing?

Do they really look like they believe that they can have the desired outcome?

If you were the universe, what would you give them?

You Can Manifest on Many Levels

Even if you don't know what you really want from life right now, you can use the law of attraction to eventually get you there. You see, life is a journey, and it's the process of creating that makes life fun and interesting.

We are creative beings and we live to create. It's natural for us to want more from life with each creation.

The law of attraction can be used for all of the things you desire. You can use it to fulfil your life purpose. If you're not sure what that is yet then use it to find your life purpose.

It can be used to improve your health, relationships, lifestyle and finances. It can be used for big things and little things. The possibilities are as infinite as the universe itself.

One of the best ways to become good at magic is to practise every day. Try it on small things. Use it to plan out your day.

The law of attraction is your connection to the greater universe. It can be a wonderful way of just connecting to the divine source. It's a practical tool and it's also a way of life.

The key to making the law of attraction work for you is to know what your subconscious programming is in relation to what you want. Otherwise, you are going to face resistance which will hamper your magnetism.

The Universe will mirror your strongest intention. Your intentions are influenced by your beliefs. You may be surprised to find out what your strongest beliefs are and where they are stored.

From Belief to Knowing and Trusting

To become successful at consciously creating requires that we follow a process. That process is simple enough but the difficulty is in really knowing, in our very being, that what we are wanting is going to happen.

I'm not going to use the word "believe" here because it's been overused and it's too difficult to achieve. Beliefs are really just thoughts that we keep habitually thinking.

The law of attraction works regardless of whether we believe it works or not. As I have said before, you are already creating your reality.

The feeling here is more of a deep knowing that it has already happened. You just **KNOW** that what you want is already in your life even though it hasn't physically manifested yet.

Now when I say, "know", I don't mean intellectual knowledge. It has nothing to do with what you intellectually know. It's not factual or even logical.

This kind of knowledge is a much higher level of knowing and it is linked to your intuition and feeling. So, forget about believing it's going to happen and rely more on your inner knowing that it's already happened.

Inner knowing can be likened to trust. When you trust someone, you just know that they are going to do the right thing by you. Knowing that the desire is already in your reality, just not physically here, is trusting.

The key to it all is trust. It's really about trusting the universe and your own subconscious mind to deliver what you want to you.

The ability to trust can become difficult when limiting beliefs are embedded in your subconscious mind. Beliefs such as lack, scarcity, unworthiness and doubt block deliberate creation.

Limiting beliefs actually cause you to attract what you don't want into your life. Even if you do manage to get something you want, these beliefs can sabotage your success at keeping it or using it to your advantage.

Do you have any of the following beliefs?

I'm not good enough.

I don't deserve to have what I want.

There isn't enough to go around.

I don't have what it takes to do this.

We'll deal with these limiting beliefs in a later chapter but for now just be aware that these beliefs are contributing to your current reality. They will contribute to your future reality too, unless you do something about them.

This trust in the universe and trust in ourselves allows us to detach from the outcome of what we want. Being able to detach from the outcome of what we want is crucial to its manifestation.

While we remain emotionally attached to the outcome, we actually project doubt into the universe. Instead, it should be a feeling of expectation and trust that it will come at the right time.

The way to gain this trust and knowing is by changing those limiting beliefs and the way to do that is to reprogram your subconscious mind.

CHAPTER TWO

Spotlight on the Mind

The Duality of the Mind

In order to change your programming and attract the life you want, it helps to understand how your mind is working. Once you begin to understand how it works then you can begin to change it.

The way you think influences your behaviour and the choices you make which affect your life in all areas. If you want more wealth, better relationships and health then your mind needs to be programmed favourably toward these things.

Our beliefs about wealth, relationships and health have been programmed into us as soon as we emerge into this physical life. Over the course of our childhood we are brainwashed by family, teachers, society and our peers.

Some of this brainwashing is helpful but a lot of it is also limiting. It's not always the fault of our parents, teachers and peers. They are just relaying what they were taught themselves.

Many of the programs we absorbed as we grew up were based around limitation, scarcity, hard work and conditional love.

If your earlier experiences and family environment weren't supportive of wealth, love and health, then your programming most likely won't be either. That's why it's important to change these old programs and install new ones.

Most people don't really know much about what their minds are up to and that makes it very difficult for them to be become the person they want to be and have the lifestyle they desire.

We talk about the mind as if it's part of the body. One way to think of the mind is that it's a pattern of nerve connections in your brain. It's that part of you that experiences YOU. (Dispenza, 2012)

Mind experts generally divide the mind into two components; conscious and subconscious. The conscious mind is your awareness of your present moment. It is that part of you that is aware of your own existence and your actions.

It is responsible for your analytical, logical and creative brain functions but it only controls 5% of your behaviour.

This conscious mind is your creative faculty and contains your desires and aspirations. It plays an important part in manifestation because you use it when you create positive affirmations and vision boards.

Here's how it works:

Think about something you want right now, see it in your mind's eye.

Imagine you have what you want right now.

That's your conscious mind working. Keeping your mind focused when visualising your desires takes concentration and that is what your conscious mind is good at. When you learn to use it well you will develop a stronger presence and this adds to your personal power and magnetism.

The subconscious mind is responsible for making sure all of your bodily processes are working including the beating of your heart and the expansion and contraction of your lungs. It's like a hard drive where every piece of your experience, past and present, is recorded for future reference.

Your subconscious mind habitually records programs which it runs over and over again. It's that part of your mind that is responsible for forming habits and beliefs. It runs on autopilot and is 95% responsible for your behaviour and what you attract to you.

The two minds work together so that you can be planning an important meeting or event while you're driving to work. You drive on autopilot and it is largely your subconscious mind in control behind the steering wheel.

When you recite your affirmations with your conscious mind and really feel and know them to be true then the two minds are working for you. The problem, however, is that even though you may consciously believe the affirmation, your subconscious mind doesn't, and that is where the trouble lies.

This is why it's so important to be aware of what you are thinking and feeling when you are trying to manifest what you want.

It could be that your conscious mind might want wealth but the subconscious mind is running the, "wealthy people are selfish", program that you inherited from your parents. This means that your subconscious mind will associate selfishness and greed with wealth.

If you're trying to avoid feeling selfish or greedy, then you'll also avoid the wealth simply because of this association. That automatically creates a disparity between what you want and what you'll get.

If there is incongruence between what your conscious mind is trying to create, and what your subconscious mind believes is possible, you will have conflict. You need to bring the two minds into harmony so that you can change your behaviour and environment to align with your conscious will.

The Mind as Filter

When your brain has over 2 million bits per second of information coming towards it at any one time it filters the information down so that you can focus, otherwise, you'd be way too overwhelmed to function. Fortunately, your brain has filtering systems that allow you to filter out much of the information coming at you.

This filtering system contributes significantly to your survival. When you go about your daily living you are constantly receiving stimuli from your environment. You might notice the television, the phone ringing or the neighbours arguing next door. These stimulants may cause you to think or feel in a certain way.

Instantaneously, your mind will assign a meaning to the various stimuli and you will experience an emotion. This may cause you to think that it's going to be a really crappy day or that you hate your demanding boss. You might have thoughts like, "I don't want to go to work today" or "I hate my job".

Here's how to start working with this:

Take a moment to think about what you are aware of in your environment at the moment.

What emotions are being stimulated by this environment?

This is an important exercise to do regularly because it shows you how you can become aware of what triggers you into a negative mindset. Your emotions come from the meaning you ascribe to a thought about your experience.

This exercise in awareness will develop your ability to be mindful of where your feelings are coming from. Once you have awareness you can begin the task of changing your reaction simply by choosing to reinterpret the stimuli.

It's important to be aware of how you react to things as these reactions affect your life and your energy.

Activity 2

Here's how you can begin to use this information to empower your ability to magnetise and manifest. Think about some recent experience where you achieved something. The thought might be, "I feel really good now that I've achieved such and such."

Really feel those feelings.

Now, who is the real author of those feelings?

Is it really the other person or situation?

What meaning did you give to the event?

Now try the same thing with the statement, "That person ruined my entire day".

Really feel those feelings.

Now, who is the real author of those feelings?

Is it really the other person or situation?

What meaning did you give to the event?

It's in your self-observation that you will find the hidden beliefs that are attracting things to you that you may not want.

When you stop and think about your reactions you will see how your brain runs on autopilot 95% of the time. This automatic filter is necessary in order for you to focus and not be overwhelmed by all of the information bombarding you most of the time.

Your mind is so sophisticated that it does three things to stop you from being overwhelmed by this oncoming information traffic.

First, it generalises. You generalise when you notice how an experience is similar to other experiences you've had in the past. Your perception of dogs for example, is informed by noticing certain qualities that you've experienced form other dogs.

There are many kinds of dogs but they are all dogs. People who are afraid of dogs will generally be afraid of all dogs and not just a specific breed or size of dog.

Although generalisation can be useful and very helpful to survival it also contributes to your limiting beliefs. These beliefs become so strong that they start to influence what you perceive.

You may generalise that to be wealthy you have to be born into a wealthy family. This can lead to incorrect conclusions about your ability to obtain wealth which can cause you to remain financially insecure.

When this kind of generalisation occurs, you lose your ability to be able to choose how you respond to people, events and situations.

Once you begin to see your generalisations and start to change them you will be able to exercise more choice in your life.

Often when you observe or remember an experience you will leave out various background details. This is called deletion and it occurs when you drop away portions of information about an incident. (Hoobyar, Dotz & Sanders, 1994)

Take a few moments to make the following observations:

Take notice of where your awareness is while you are reading this book.

Are there other things going on around you?

Were you aware of the other things while you were reading this book?

I know that at the moment while I am writing this, I wasn't aware that there was music playing in the background. Now that I become aware of it I'm noticing what song it is and how loud it is. Where was my awareness of it a moment ago?

This is how your mind deletes seemingly extraneous information. Doing this is important and necessary. When you visualise your goals, you will need to delete all of the information around you so you can concentrate on the details of your vision.

The final way the brain filters out information is through distortion. When your brain uses the filter of distortion, it actually changes your experience of what is occurring to a modified version of what you **BELIEVE** is happening.

This new version will usually be influenced by your generalisations about similar past experiences. In reality it is only a portion of the experience because you've edited much of the detail and filled in the rest with your imagination.

Recall a person who is afraid of dogs. They may have been bitten once by a dog but now they see all dogs as potentially dangerous. First, they have bundled all dogs into one category and secondly, they have distorted the potential of being bitten by every dog they meet.

All of these filters are necessary and work with each other. Knowing how this all works allows you to observe your own filters and change your thinking and perceptions from unhelpful ones to ones that help you achieve your potential.

Who's Running Your Show

Our subconscious mind is like a hard drive. It records programs and plays the program over and over. The only way to stop the subconscious mind from constantly replaying the programs of unworthiness, scarcity, doubt and fear is to rewrite the program.

Have you ever heard the statement that money is the root of all evil? If you believe that then no matter how hard you try to bully the subconscious into changing that belief with willpower, it won't budge.

So, who is running the show? Well it's the subconscious mind of course.

Why is it important? Well, it's running your show and

your show is your life.

Trance Junkies

Did you know that you go in and out of trance multiple times a day?

When you are driving, you're in trance. When you watch television, you're in trance. The trance state is the best state to communicate with and change the subconscious mind. That is why hypnosis is so effective. When you are in trance your critical faculty is bypassed.

As children between the ages of 1 and 6, we spent most of our waking time in a trance state. This means that we were most programmable between these ages. Many of your blocks to wealth, prosperity and fulfilling relationships originate during those early years.

Here's what you can do to start the ball rolling for change:

Read through the instructions below and then close your eyes and do it. It's really important to do the exercises in this book because magnetising is a practice.

Designing and manifesting the life you want is a practical pursuit and not just an intellectual exercise. You can't change your life via your intellect. It goes much deeper than that.

Activity 3

Think back to a time when you were between 1 and 6 years old and see yourself as that little impressionable child.

Can you remember wanting something but not being allowed to have it? Now it may have been for a very good reason at the time.

How does that little child feel about this?

Did someone say something to that little child about why she/he couldn't have it?

Was this reason given a lot?

Most importantly, what did that little girl or boy learn about the world that day?

What you learned about the world that day is what you still subconsciously believe now. This is a block to manifestation and a block to your creative and abundant life.

Another thing to be aware of is how much your subconscious is still being programmed. As I mentioned above, you go into trance every time you watch TV.

If you really want to see positive change in your life start to make changes to your vibration by asking yourself the following questions so that you can better know your mind and your vibration.

What do you watch on TV or DVD?

Is it uplifting and inspiring?

Is it full of violence, fear and aggression?

What message is the program giving you?

Your subconscious mind can't tell the difference between what is real and what is imagined. How do you think it's reacting to all of the fear and destruction it is subjected to while watching the 6 o'clock news?

We Are Suggestible Beings

Every day we are being reprogrammed by the world around us. We live in a wonderful culture but it has its downside.

When you switch on the media, what do you find?

Is it about love, joy and the wonderful things that people experience every day?

Or is it full of doom, fear and scarcity?

Next time you watch or listen to the media, especially the news, ask yourself what the main emotional trigger is.

Really look for it and become aware of it. This is going into your suggestible subconscious mind over and over, day after day.

Is this helping you achieve the life you actually want or is it just keeping you stuck?

These are very important questions to ask yourself if you want to move forward with your life in a happy and joyful way.

It may seem as if I'm asking you to bury your head in the sand. The truth is that you're probably going to find out about something important even if you don't watch the news. Someone will surely tell you about it.

This is something to think about if you're serious about trying to create your own new world of peace and abundance. If you want peace and abundance then you need to spend the majority of your time immersing yourself in things that reflect peace and abundance.

You don't need to give up watching the news entirely, just observe how much of your life is taken up with things that enhance fear and struggle compared to things that promote abundance and wellbeing. Then try to tip the scales in favour of abundance and well-being.

Sound selfish, well yes, it is. Think about this. You

can't be poor enough to help the most impoverished person out of their poverty. You can't get sick enough to heal a sick person.

The only way you can change the world in a global fashion is to work on your own world first. Think of the warning the airlines give parents if there is an emergency. They tell the parents to put the oxygen on themselves first and then the child.

You need to raise your own vibration before you can influence the world around you.

Suggestibility is not all bad. In fact, it is because we are so suggestible that we are able to make the changes we need to our programming.

Suggestibility plays an important role in our ability to learn and is necessary for our survival. We just need to be selective about what kind of suggestions we allow our subconscious mind to absorb.

The Mind and the Matrix

It might be helpful to think of your brain as an antenna that transmits and receives information to and from a much larger universal field. Your brain has its own magnetic field which interacts with this universal field. This universal field mirrors your thoughts and beliefs.

What you send out you get back. You may not get exactly what you've sent out but you will get some version of it.

Your thoughts dictate your emotions and your emotions reinforce your thoughts. It's a loop. Your energy is directly affected by your thoughts and emotions. This energy is what you are sending out into the universal field. This field connects all life and is a matrix of energy.

You are constantly communicating with this field. It's like cause and effect but without any judgement. The universe gives back what you put out. The problem is this; you don't know what you're really putting out there until you start to observe your thinking and behaviour.

What energy are you putting out to the universe today?

The Heart and the Magnet

We can't talk about magnetism without mentioning the powerful size of the magnetic field emanating from the heart.

Your heart generates the largest magnetic field in your body. In fact, the magnetic field of the heart is 60 times greater in amplitude than the brain's field when recorded on an electroencephalogram (EEG).

Research has shown that when two people touch or are in close proximity to each other electromagnetic energy is exchanged between them.

Studies are showing that the heart's magnetic field contains information or coding that is transmitted outside of the body. It seems that emotions influence this information and when we change our emotions, we also change the coding.

The information contained in this field has the ability to affect people and animals around us. So, what else does it affect around us?

Can you recall a really positive experience you had with someone you love recently?

What does the area around you heart feel like when

you remember this relationship?

I do this little experiment when I'm out walking. When I walk past a house that has a barking dog in the front garden, I consciously focus strong feelings of joy toward it.

I like dogs so it's easy for me to express appreciation when I see one. Most dogs will stop barking and look somewhat confused and some even start wagging their tails. Dogs are very social animals and respond extremely well to heartfelt joy and love.

The Mind and Heart Work Together

The ultimate goal is to have the heart and mind working together so that our thoughts are producing the positive emotions that we want in order to communicate abundance, prosperity and harmony to the universal field.

Let's look at this more closely so you can develop your skills of self-observation further.

Think about something you've always wanted but have never achieved. Maybe it's something you've even given up on.

What are your thoughts about it?

How do these thoughts make you feel?

We'll come back to this later when we start to work with those limiting beliefs but for now just be aware of your thoughts and feelings about the things you want.

Examine the difference between the thoughts and feelings concerning the things you want and receive, and the thoughts and feeling about the things you just don't seem to be able to attract.

The aim is for you to easily choose to think supportive and helpful thoughts rather than ones that limit and don't support your goals.

CHAPTER THREE

Get with The Program

Our Subconsious Programs

When we give our attention to something we connect with it emotionally. If you want more money, your thoughts and emotions will be connected to that desire.

Your thoughts govern your behaviour and your actions. These thoughts and actions have an influence on the people around you. This is because you are sending out energetic information into your environment, which affects what you experience in return.

It's not a case of sending the wrong message out to the universe either. It's also about sending the wrong message more locally as well. Everything is connected, so what you give your attention to will affect everything around you.

When you give your attention to something like your bank account for example, you will likely experience thoughts and feelings about it. These thoughts will cause you to view your bank account in a particular way.

If your thoughts are negative then looking at your bank account will most likely bring up feelings of fear and dread. Your attention to these feelings will reinforce what you believe about your money situation and about money in general. Consequently, this will only reinforce your subconscious program about your relationship with money.

What kind of messages are you sending out?

What kind of response are you receiving?

What you believe is so important to the quality of your life that it's imperative that you learn to really understand your beliefs. It's even more important to dig down and know what your subconscious beliefs are because they are running the show.

I keep repeating this, but it's important that you really learn this. Your subconscious beliefs are the most important beliefs you have. It's time to start making them work for you.

Your beliefs affect how you behave. If you believe that you don't deserve to be wealthy then you will act that way. Other people will perceive this attitude in you and treat you that way. This extends out into the universe.

The universe and people are like a mirror. They simply feed back to you what you perceive both in yourself and your environment.

Take the time to really think about the following questions in relation to money.

Does money flow to you easily and effortlessly?

What is your financial situation like?

How would you describe your feelings toward your job?

What kind of job do you have?

You can do the same with relationships:

Do you find it easy to form loving and lasting relationships?

What are your current relationships like?

How would you describe your feelings toward your current relationship?

The answers to these questions will give you an indication of what messages you are sending out to other people and the universe. I encourage you to answer them as honestly as you can.

You experience what you perceive. If you perceive yourself to be hopeless with managing money then you will be. If you perceive yourself as unattractive and unworthy of another person's love then you will be.

I am not suggesting that you don't have the skills or worth. It's more about how you're acting and behaving. The universe will take notice of what you feel about yourself and send you more of it.

How to find Your Programs

To find your programs, you need to ask yourself some questions. I know that it can be very hard to know what your blocks actually are. The following two activities will help you begin to find your limiting beliefs.

Activity 4

Below is a series of statements which focus on the most common beliefs that people have about themselves and world. You may already be aware of some of these beliefs and some of them you may not be aware of. Make sure that you answer these questions honestly.

I never finish what I start.

I'm not an expert.

Why would anyone listen to me?
I'm not good enough.
I didn't work hard enough.
I don't have time.
People will judge me poorly.
I'll sound stupid.
No one cares about me or my ideas.
No one in my family has ever achieved that.
I don't know enough.
I'm too old.
I'm too young.
I don't deserve to be wealthy.
I don't deserve to be happy.
I don't deserve to have the lifestyle I want.
I can't because I have kids.
I'm scared of being rejected.
I can't do that.
I'm too shy.
My family won't approve.

Now that you have found some limiting beliefs, let's see how they limit your vision of your future.

Activity 5

Close your eyes and imagine a scene where you are totally living your full potential.

Imagine the environment you are in, the people you are with, and the amount of money you are earning.

Take notice of what you're wearing and what you're

doing.

Spend a few minutes in this scene as if you are living it now.

How do you feel about this vision?

Does it feel comfortable or uncomfortable?

What emotions do you feel?

Does it feel like it really could happen or that it's just wishful thinking?

What thoughts come into your mind?

Write down your feelings, both good and bad, and then take a look at the list of statements again.

Do some of your feelings correspond to some of those beliefs?

I bet there were some limiting beliefs and uncomfortable feelings that came out of the previous activities.

By the way, please make sure that you do these activities. You won't be able to progress toward you dreams and desires unless you take action.

In order to be a powerful magnet to what you want you have to know yourself. You can't just skim over the uncomfortable feelings and doubts as they will sabotage your success.

Success depends on knowing where your blocks are. If you can get to the point where you don't think those limiting thoughts anymore, then you will find that making money, improving your well being, and attracting wonderful relationships can become your reality.

Your Unique Energy Signature

The previous activities should have made you aware

of some of your energy blocks. These emotions and thoughts help create your unique energy signature. Of course, your empowering thoughts and feelings also contribute to your unique energy signature.

Quantum physicists have been able to prove that atoms are made up of 99.9% energy. Your unique energy signature is the electromagnetic charge that is unique to you (Dispenza, 2012).

All atoms vibrate and when they come together, they share their vibration. It's much like guitar strings that are tuned to the same note, they will vibrate together.

You are made up of atoms. Everything is made of atoms.

When you are in a joyous and positive emotional state you will resonate with people and situations that resonate at a similar frequency to you. Likewise, when you are feeling angry, fearful, or ashamed, you will resonate with people and situations that are an energetic vibration to those emotions.

Next time you're out in public, take a look around you at all of the people you pass by. Find a shopping mall somewhere and just sit and watch the people around you.

Notice how they walk, what they're wearing and their posture. What expressions do they have on their faces?

We can learn a lot about energy signatures from observing the "vibes" that we get from other people. While you're people watching, just think about what kind of beliefs and thoughts these people may have about themselves.

Our posture, sense of dress and gait are clues to what

we are thinking about ourselves and our relationship to the world around us.

Now you've heard all of the theory and know how your mind works. You are also starting to see your limiting beliefs. It's now time to get to know and change these beliefs about yourself and your ability to attract what you want to you.

PART TWO

TAPPING INTO EMPOWERMENT

Until recently, there were very few quick and effective ways to change the programs in our brain. However, over the last 30 years there have been an astounding number of techniques that have been producing amazing results. Thanks to the internet, these techniques are beginning to be more widely known and applied.

Emotional Freedom Technique (EFT) is one such technology that is hitting the world by storm. People are beginning to apply it in all manner of ways and are seeing amazing results within a reasonably short space of time.

You're going to learn that technique and apply it so that you can magnetise your life and start designing your future.

I was first introduced to EFT when I was going through a very stressful stage in my life. I was suffering from anxiety and insomnia. Although I went through a process of hypnotherapy for the anxiety, I also started using EFT.

I would have to say that EFT was actually more effective in the long term than hypnotherapy. I love it and believe that is definitely one of the quickest and most effective brain retraining modalities in our world today.

What I didn't know, until I starting learning to be an EFT practitioner, was that this powerful brain changer can also be used as a powerful manifestation technique.

Once you really know what it is you want and acknowledge your own potential, you will find that you will be using this technique almost every day. So, let's begin!

CHAPTER FOUR

Change Your Energy Signature

Energy Psychology, Energy Change

Emotional Freedom Technique (EFT) is also known as just Tapping. It falls under the Umbrella term, Energy Psychology.

EFT is very similar to acupressure meridian therapy. You simply use two or three fingers to tap on various meridian points on the body while concentrating on what you are feeling and thinking.

It's really that simple. The tapping balances the energy meridians that become blocked or disrupted when we are feeling negative emotion and limiting beliefs.

EFT is currently being researched, and the results from randomised trials have been quite encouraging.

Researches who have conducted trails based on meridian therapies have found that applying pressure on various points has a calming effect on the Amygdala, the flight or fight centre of the brain.

This technique has been used extensively to help people recover from anxiety, post-traumatic stress disorder and other various emotional disorders with extreme success.

EFT has been able to help these people when other forms of therapy failed. Please do some research about this as there is a lot of information out there regarding the powerful benefits of EFT.

So how will this help you reach your potential and manifest the life you want?

Your potential is directly affected by your perceptions about yourself, the external world around you and your place in this world.

EFT can help you change these perceptions.

If your subconscious mind is running a program that is limiting you, then you can use EFT to rewrite the program.

This is because the technique of Tapping places you into a slight trance state. In this state, you can directly access your subconscious mind.

So, I'm going to ask you again to do some thinking about something you want but don't think you can have. It can be the same thing as in previous activities.

Notice how you feel!

That's the result of a stimulus (what you're thinking about) and an emotional result. This is very important. Your feelings are your guidance system and help you determine if something isn't congruent with what you want.

Where do you feel that emotion physically in your body?

Yes, we feel our emotions in our body. If we didn't have a body, we wouldn't know we were having an emotion.

So, you've got a desire and a contradictory belief in

your subconscious mind. This belief is causing an uncomfortable feeling in your body. This uncomfortable feeling in your body will reinforce the belief in your subconscious.

It's like a feedback loop between the mind and body.

If I see a snake on the path, my instinct tells my body that something is dangerous, my body reacts with an uncomfortable sensation and the discomfort sends a signal to the brain that I'm feeling fear.

Once the brain identifies the fear it sends a message to my body that the snake is dangerous causing me to react. This mind/body cycle will reinforce the belief in the subconscious mind that snakes are dangerous.

The problem is that if I see anything that looks like a snake on the path, like a long stick or a harmless lizard, I will initially react the same way.

I've seen far more lizards and sticks than I have snakes, but when I see a long squiggly thing on a path, I will probably react to it as if it were a snake first. That will continue to happen until I interrupt that mind/body pattern.

EFT is a powerful pattern interrupting technique. I'll show you how it's done.

Tapping into Change

If you've never tried tapping before, or have never experienced acupuncture, then you may find tapping a little odd. Once you experience the effects, you will hopefully think otherwise.

So, let's start with the basic process.

Use this video link below to learn how to tap.

https://youtu.be/ECAKO5-49j0

Follow the tapping video by using either two or three fingers to lightly tap on each point. You can use one hand or two hands, one on each side of the body.

Point No. 1 is the eyebrow point. It's located between your two eyebrows. Actually, the points are at the beginning of the eyebrow on both sides.

Point No. 2 is on the bone at the side of the eyes. Don't tap in the eyes, just tap on the bone.

Point No. 3 is on the bone directly under the eyes.

Point No. 4 is under the nose. It's between the nose and the top lip.

Point No. 5 is in that indentation between the lower lip and your chin.

Point No. 6 is just under the collar bone on both sides.

Point No. 7 is about 4 inches under the arm. For women it's where your bra line starts.

There is another point called the *karate chop point* and that is located on the outside of the palm of either hand. This point is used at the beginning of a tapping session and I'll show you how it is used when we begin tapping.

Ok, you know where to tap so now what!

Most people don't know what to say or really do when they first start. Throughout this book I will be providing you with scripts for each tapping point. This is just to get you started and comfortable with the method.

The important thing is to connect to whatever emotion comes up for you while you are tapping. You need to know what the emotion is and where you are feeling it in your body so you can change it.

Now, this is where a lot of people get confused when

it comes to the law of attraction and expressing negative feelings. We know that in order to raise our magnetic vibration we need to focus on the positive and be happy and joyful. So, doesn't focusing on our negative feelings contradict this?

It may seem like a contradiction and it is in a way. But here's the thing - you can't get to positive, happy and joyful from negative, sad and miserable without doing something in between.

When you do EFT, you are only temporarily focusing on the negative while you clear away the blocked energy. Think of it this way. You can't have clean dishes until you see the dirt that's on them first and then wash it away.

Once you've cleared the negative emotions you can begin to reprogram your subconscious mind with positive programs. Yes, you can use EFT for that too.

Let's Begin!

One of the main reasons people often fail to achieve what they want is because they subconsciously have something to gain from limiting themselves.

I know that this may sound crazy. Why would someone deliberately sabotage their success? This comes back to our programming, usually in our childhood, when it may have been safer for us to limit ourselves.

Unfortunately, we continue with that limitation throughout adulthood until we change it. This is called secondary gain or psychological reversal.

I have a friend who was incredibly brilliant at music. He would have been a successful musician but whenever he would begin to have some success something would happen to block the flow. So, he developed a habit of procrastinating. He would attract situations and other work to do so he didn't have time for his music.

One day I asked him what he feared the most about achieving his dream of being a successful musician. He told me that he really didn't feel like he could handle the responsibilities that come with success. So instead of attracting success, he was attracting failure because that's what he subconsciously believed he deserved. The universe heard him and delivered failure every time.

People will hold their secondary gain in place for many reasons. Below is a list of some secondary benefits. Read them and notice if some of them resonate with you.

Not feeling safe to change.

Feeling like you don't deserve to have what you want.

Feeling like your identity will change if you achieve what it is you want and that makes you feel uncomfortable.

Friends and family may react to you in negative ways if you achieve what it is that you want.

Do you believe having what you want goes against your spiritual beliefs?

When we start tapping, we acknowledge this resistance. By acknowledging our resistance, we are telling our subconscious mind that we are aware of the resistance. This enables us to release it so that we can continue removing the limiting beliefs and emotions around the issue.

The way we do it is through what EFT practitioners call the *Basic Recipe*. The Basic Recipe is the basic procedure used to treat any emotional issue with EFT.

Tapping in Action

Remember those limiting beliefs you explored in Activity 1. Well, I'm going to choose one of the most common ones and use that to show you how EFT works. The limiting belief is going to be, "I'm not good enough."

This is one of the most common beliefs that prevent the law of attraction from working. Many people feel they don't have what it takes to make their dreams and desires happen. Unfortunately, all of our thoughts, feelings and behaviours are the result of the beliefs we formed in our childhood.

Did you ever hear the following comments while you were growing up?

Don't take too much because there might not be enough.
Are you sure you can do that?
You did it wrong.
Can't you do anything right?
It's not safe to do that alone.
No one is interested in that.
Who do you think you are?
No one in our family ever achieved that.
Don't go thinking you're better than me.
You're just like your mother/father.
You can't do that.

Even if we aren't directly told these things we pick them up through mirroring other people's behaviour.

I picked up a lot of my mother's feelings of unworthiness and not being good enough simply by observing her.

She expressed that belief through her words and actions.

When we are children, we internalise the behaviour of the adults around us subconsciously. It's how we learn. We learn by copying. Unfortunately, we don't only copy the useful behaviours, we copy the limiting ones as well.

It's not necessarily your parents' fault. They were most probably doing the best they could. Many of the limiting beliefs were communicated to us with the best of intentions.

So, here's how it works:

If you feel that you're not good enough to have a loving relationship, then the universe will take you at your word and you won't get that loving relationship. You might find that you become attracted to people who don't treat you the way you want to be treated. This may be because your subconscious mind believes you don't deserve better.

If you feel you aren't good enough or don't have what it takes to run a successful business then you may stay in a job where you feel unfulfilled.

Activity 6

I want you to say this out loud, "I'm not good enough." Really sense how that makes you feel. Become aware of where you are feeling that in your body. Many people feel it either in their chest area or in the belly.

Now how does that belief make you feel emotionally?

Where in your body do you feel it?

Write your feelings down and rate them from 0 to 10, with 0 being calm and 10 representing the most intense and uncomfortable feeling ever.

When you say, "I'm not good enough", rate that on the scale from 0 to 10, with 0 being it feels completely false to 10 being completely true.

Tap on the side of your hand at the karate chop point and say the following while feeling that uncomfortable feeling.

Karate Chop: Even though I believe I'm not good enough, I deeply and completely accept myself.

Karate Chop: Even though I feel anxious when I think about how I'm not good enough, I choose to change this now.

Karate Chop: Even though I really believe I'm not good enough, I'm going to honour this feeing anyway.

Now tap on the following points, just like on the diagram, and say the words written next to them below. Tap about 5 to 10 times on each point.

Eyebrow point: I'm not good enough.

Side of the Eye: I'm just not good enough.

Under the Eye: I feel like I'm not good enough.

Under the Nose: This makes me anxious.

Above the Chin: Fearful.

Collarbone: I've always felt like I'm just not good enough.

Under the Arm: It's been that way for a long time.

Eyebrow point: It's like I've never been good enough.

Side of the Eye: I just can't seem to shift that feeling.

Under the Eye: Feeling like I'm just not good enough.

Under the Nose: I'm scared that I'll fail because I'm not good enough.

Above the Chin: I feel anxious that I'm not good enough.

Collarbone: If I'm not good enough, I can't succeed.

Under the Arm: And that scares me.

Eyebrow point: I'm telling myself that I'm not good enough.

Side of the Eye: Yes, that's right! I'm telling myself that I'm not good enough.

Under the Eye: I'll just keep telling myself that I'm not good enough.

Under the Nose: It feels safe to believe I'm not good enough.

Above the Chin: I'm not offending other people when I'm not good enough.

Collarbone: I can be the nice person when I'm not good enough.

Under the Arm: I don't have to stand out when I'm not good enough.

Eyebrow point: This is crazy!

Side of the Eye: Who told me I'm not good enough?

Under the Eye: I'm now telling me that I'm not good enough.

Under the Nose: Not being good enough scares me.

Above the Chin: I feel anxious that I'm not good enough.

Collarbone: I'm too afraid to succeed.

Under the Arm: Because I'm telling myself that I'm just not good enough.

Eyebrow point: But what if I was good enough?

Side of the Eye: What if I was at least a little better than I thought?

Under the Eye: What if I'm wrong about me?

Under the Nose: It's very possible that I am wrong about me?

Above the Chin: I'm could be just running an old program.

Collarbone: That my subconscious mind recorded a long time ago.

Under the Arm: Probably when I was a child.

Eyebrow point: My subconscious mind is just running the same old program.

Side of the Eye: Over and over again.

Under the Eye: What if I changed the program?

Under the Nose: It's very possible that it's wrong about me.

Above the Chin: I could just change the program.

Collarbone: But that just seems so hard right now.

Under the Arm: I'm just so used to feeling like I'm not good enough.

Now take a nice deep breath and relax. Check in with yourself and see how you are feeling.

Use the scale from 0 to 10 to see if your feelings have changed.

Say aloud, "I'm not good enough", and connect with how that feels.

Does it feel as true as it did before you started tapping? Or does it feel less true or even false?

You can rate how true it feels on the 0 to 10 scale too, with 0 being false and 10 being true.

If you're position on the scale is above 3 do that whole tapping round again. Keep doing it until you get to a 3 or less.

Once you hit 3 or less on the scale do the following tapping script:

Eyebrow point: That's right I'm just running an old program.

Side of the Eye: And programs can be changed.

Under the Eye: How willing am I to change this limiting belief?

Under the Nose: It's about time I changed the program.

Above the Chin: It's about time I stop telling me I'm not good enough.

Collarbone: I'm just going to honour myself and how I feel right now.

Under the Arm: I'm going to work toward changing this limiting belief.

Eyebrow point: What if I am good enough?

Side of the Eye: What if I do deserve success?

Under the Eye: I'm willing to believe it's possible.

Under the Nose: I'm willing to believe that I am good enough.

Above the Chin: I'm willing to believe that I am good enough to succeed.

Collarbone: I'm just going to honour that willingness.

Under the Arm: I'm going to see this as an opportunity to change my relationship with me.

Eyebrow point: I choose to change my beliefs about me.

Side of the Eye: I can step up and follow my desire.

Under the Eye: I'm choosing to make friends with myself.

Under the Nose: I'm choosing to believe that I am worthy.

Above the Chin: I'm choosing to believe that I have what it takes to succeed.

Collarbone: Even if I need a little help and training now and then.

Under the Arm: I'm choosing to believe in me and my worthiness to succeed.

Take a deep breath and relax.

Check in with how you feel and rate that on the 0 to 10 scale.

Say out loud, "I'm not good enough", and see how true that is now.

If you're down to a 0 then you can relax and move on. If you're still around a 2 or 3 repeat the process above until you're at least down to a 1.

So that's an example of how EFT works.

You might find that as you are tapping that other thoughts and feelings come up for you. You can write those down and tap on them later following the above process.

We always start the tapping process focusing on the negative and then once the feelings start to subside, we start to flip the process around toward the positive.

This is the beginning of how EFT can be used to remove blocks and steer you towards manifesting what you want.

That's not all though. We'll be covering how EFT is used to change your life from one of reaction to a life by design.

CHAPTER FIVE

Knowing What You Want

What's Your Current Story?

We tell ourselves stories all the time. Each and every one of us has many stories stored in our subconscious mind. Most of the time we're not even aware that we tell stories about the world, ourselves and others.

Our mind is constantly active. It's like a monkey swinging from tree to tree. We have quiet dialogue running on autopilot in our heads all of the time.

Becoming aware of what we are thinking is so important because it influences what we magnetise into our lives. Most of us tell ourselves stories about lack, doubt, unworthiness and fear.

This isn't surprising given that we're constantly exposing ourselves to these stories through the media and people around us.

It's now time to start becoming aware of what you are thinking by learning to listen to your internal dialogue.

We're not taught any of this at school, yet knowing how we think and what stories we tell ourselves determines what actions we take in life and what actions we don't take. Our stories influence how we live our lives and what choices we make.

These choices include romantic partners, career, income level, and what we consume. All of these choices are determined by our subconscious beliefs about ourselves and the way we should live our lives.

The only way to know what stories you are telling yourself is to slow down and listen. You might be surprised at some of the things you tell yourself about you.

This next activity will provide you with an opportunity to observe just how much you think and how your thinking is constant.

Activity 7

Spend 3 minutes observing what you are thinking. The easiest way to do this is to try to NOT think for 3 minutes. You'll soon become aware of how much your mind wants to think!

Could you catch those thoughts?

What were they?

If you can't remember what you were thinking, try the exercise again. This time, write down what you are thinking about or trying not to think about as you are doing the exercise.

That inner dialogue is constantly chattering away throughout your day. Only you're not aware of it most of the time.

Becoming aware of your thoughts is really important because it's these thoughts that the universe is mirroring. But don't panic. It's not like you can't have a negative thought.

Negative thoughts let you know that you need to pay

attention to something that's going on in your life. They are your guidance system and they play an important role in your life. They are actually necessary, so don't get hung up on having a negative emotion.

You could think of negative thoughts and feelings as a signal that something isn't the way you want it to be and then do something about it. As you get used to observing yourself and practising EFT every day, you will be able to quickly find the cause and then make the change.

So, what do I mean when I say that we all tell ourselves stories?

Have you ever worked with someone who complains a lot?

You know someone who moans and groans about all the work they have to do, how they barely earn enough to make ends meet and they criticise everything and everyone.

Well, I've worked with people like that. I'll tell you a story about one of them. Annika has a clerical job in a major corporation. Annika isn't happy. No one likes her because she is always complaining about her workload and other people. She's never satisfied. She always moans about not having any money. She has a "woe is me" attitude.

What story do you think Annika is telling herself every day?

Well, it's like this.

"I've got to go to work because I need the money. I don't like my job. They give me too much work. I'm sure I do more work around here than most people. If only I didn't need the money and it's not enough anyway. Other people have it so much easier than me."

Annika tells herself that story throughout the whole day, every day. She is actually subconsciously attached to her suffering and her life just seems to be getting harder and harder.

Annika is focusing on what she doesn't want. The Universe will mirror what she's thinking about the most, therefore, it will give her more of the same.

Here's what the universe is hearing:

have to work

not enough money

a job I don't like

too much work

more work than others

it's hard for me

So, Annika is saying, "Dear Universe, I want to have to work. I want less money than I need. I want a job that I hate and lots of work. I want to do more work than others. I want it to be hard."

Please ask yourself the following questions:

What story are you telling yourself regarding your current work and/or financial situation?

What story are you telling yourself about your current relationships?

Activity 8

Pick an area of your life that you want to change and write a story about it. Once you've written down a paragraph or two, dot point what you think you are telling the universe. You can use the story above as a guideline.

How many limiting thoughts or statements can you

find in your story?

How many positive thoughts or statements can you find in your story?

Are the following thoughts or beliefs a part of your story?

1. *scarcity*
2. *doubt*
3. *fear*
4. *unworthiness*
5. *not good enough*

The above activity will help you become aware of your limiting thoughts and beliefs which surround that desire. It's important that you do this so you can begin to change your thinking and hence change your ability to attract what you desire.

What Don't You Want?

Can you see from the previous exercise how you are telling the universe what it is you **DON'T** want? Your subconscious mind doesn't understand negatives. So it cancels out the "don't" and only hears "I want". The universe does the same. That's why we always use positive words in affirmations.

The good news is, that one of the best ways to find out what you really want is to know what you don't want.

Try the following activity.

Activity 9

Think about what you don't want and write it all down. Do a brain dump about what you don't want. Leave space next to each item so that you can write something next to it later.

For example: I hate my job, it's so boring.

Don't panic, the universe isn't going to suddenly make all of these things happen because you're focusing on them. The universe honours the intention and your intention right now is to identify what's been blocking you from manifesting your desire so that you can change it.

As I've said before, you can't clean dirty dishes if you can't see the dirt. So go on now and write down those things you just don't want in your life any longer.

Finding What You Do Want

Now you're going to find out what you do want.

Let's get back to your brain dump.

Activity 10

Look over your list of items that you don't want in your life. Next to each item that you've written down write down what you do want instead.

Everything that you don't want contains the essence of something that you do want.

For example: I hate my job because it's so boring. I'd like a job where I can use my creativity and design skills.

Writing down what you don't want is a great way to find out what you actually want. Sometimes we get so caught up with thinking about what we hate and don't want in our lives that we forget to even entertain thoughts about what we'd like in its place.

When I've asked people what they want, many of

them just can't tell me. It's no wonder that they're not feeling happy and fulfilled. The universe is only receiving information about what they don't want. It's not receiving any information about what they would prefer.

So do the activities above and you'll find out more about what you really want. This will help you steer your life toward what will bring you more joy and fulfilment.

We're going to continue with your story in a minute, but first I would like to tell you a story that illustrates how we can change our stories from being limiting and negative to being positive and supportive.

Leila doesn't want to drive her beat up old car anymore. It's very old and it looks really shabby. As Leila thinks about the car, she desires a new car.

Leila isn't telling herself a story about her nice new car. Instead Leila is telling herself the story about her old shabby one.

Leila says: "I hate my old car. It's so shabby. How I wish I could afford a new one. I'm dreaming. Nobody in my family has ever owned a brand-new car. How could I ever afford something like that? I hate having to drive an old car. What must people think? I'm embarrassed about my car."

Leila's story isn't very positive. Her focus points are:

hate car

old car

shabby car

not enough money

have to drive old car

So, is Leila asking the universe for an old shabby car

that she hates? In fact she insists that she "has to drive an old car".

How can Leila change this story?

Leila could say something like this: "My old car has served me and I appreciate it and now I'd like a new car. I really enjoy having a car that I can rely on. I love the way that new cars smell. Oh, I think I'd like a red one. I really appreciate the feeling I have when I sit behind the wheel of a new car. I'm looking forward to my new car. I thank the universe for bringing me a new shiny red car and doing this for me."

Leila's new focus points are:

I want a car that serves me

I want a new car

I want a reliable car

I want a shiny car

I'd like a red car

I want it really shiny

I'd love a new car

I deserve that new car

Now it's time for you to write your new story.

Activity 11

Now write your new story. Don't worry if you feel like a fake. Don't worry if it feels silly. Just try it. The new story may not "fit" the image you have of yourself at the moment and that's OK, just do the activity.

I'd really like you to acknowledge the thoughts and feelings you are having as you write down your new story. Write them down as they come up for you and we'll begin tapping on them in the next chapter.

The Essence of What You Want

Great, you have your new story! Now it's time to find the essence of it. By essence I mean the deeper reason for why you want it. There can be positive and negative reasons here.

Why do people want money?

Well, you can buy things you want. You can pay the rent or mortgage. With money you can buy food and clothing. Having a substantial amount of money in the bank can make you feel secure. Money is crucial for survival.

Money can make life much easier. Instead of having to do things yourself that you may find difficult or just don't like doing, you can pay someone else to do it for you. Health requirements are more easily met with money.

When it comes to money it's usually about security. Being able to pay the rent and put food on the table helps us feel safe. Without money we can feel afraid for our very survival.

Feeling safe is surely better than feeling frightened and insecure all of the time. Whatever the reason for wanting more money is, you can bet there is an emotional need underlying it.

Not knowing the essence of what you want or the "why" of what you want can sabotage your magnetism, especially if it is associated with a limiting belief. Your subconscious mind will be focusing on the negative belief instead of the desire because that will be what is dominant in its programming.

Let's revisit Leila's story again in order to make this

clearer.

Leila wants a new car but if she wants one because she feels embarrassed driving the older car then she will need to deal with that feeling of not being good enough first.

This is because she's sending a message to the universe that she's not good enough. The universe will respond by giving her more of the same. In her case it's an old car.

The positive side is that she might really enjoy the feel of a nice new car. If Leila can remove the belief about not being good enough, she will have a greater chance of getting that new car.

Drawing Out the Essence

When I wanted to go into business for myself, I felt that it was a way that I could fully live my potential. I also wanted to work on my terms and not have an organisation dictate my life.

I wanted to do what I enjoyed and help people in a way that was of real benefit to them. I did the following exercise to see what the essence of my desire to work for myself was.

When I'm working for myself, I'll feel totally free. This means that I can do what I most enjoy in life and use my skills and talents to actualise my real potential and I'll be able prove to my family that I am good enough to do it my way.

Now I'm going to dot point the essence of my desire to work for myself.

totally free

do what I most enjoy

use my skills and talents
actualise my potential
self-worth

Wow, so that's what I really want?

My business then becomes a vehicle for me to do what I most enjoy in life while using my skills and talents to achieve my potential.

The most interesting point here is what I feel I need to prove to my family. You're probably wondering why the idea of proving it to someone is included.

We often do things or want things due to an unconscious drive to seek some kind of approval from our parents, family and friends. It's so unconscious that we don't always know that it's there. That's why it's included in the essence finding strategy.

If we are doing things because we need to prove ourselves then we are doing these things for limiting reasons. This won't help us feel that joy in life when we do achieve our desire because we will always be looking for approval from someone else.

Knowing this was important for me because it meant that I still needed to do some work on self-acceptance and self-approval.

What I needed to do was to work on my feelings relating to my potential, and self-worth before I could manifest my business. If I don't feel like I'm living my potential and I don't feel worthy now, then I won't feel the way I need to feel to run a successful business. Get it!

Try this for yourself.

Activity 12

Go back to your story and fill answer the questions below:

1. Name your desire.
2. How will achieving it make you feel?
3. What will achieving your desire mean for you?
4. Are you seeking approval from anyone?
5. Who will you be when you achieve your desire?

The above exercise will expose the real reasons underlying why you want what you want. We'll begin to tap on the essence of what you want in the next chapter.

PART THREE

Program Upgrade

When I first started practising EFT, I was surprised by some of my beliefs about myself and my capabilities. I found that the tapping process produced a lot of clarity about the way I perceived the world and my relationship to it.

My inner critic and my limited beliefs were often quite shocking, and most of them I could trace back to my childhood.

It wasn't just the things I had been told either. I realised that I was mirroring the adults in my family. I adopted their limited beliefs about their capabilities and applied them to myself.

In this section you are going to be doing a lot of tapping on your limiting beliefs and you may find that most of them come from your upbringing as well.

Once the negative beliefs are out of the way, you can focus on what you want with a stronger resolve that will be supported by your subconscious mind. You can cement new beliefs into your subconscious so that the conscious work you do will have a greater affect.

While you're waiting for the universe to bring you the life you'd like, you'll need to appreciate the one you already have. Otherwise, the universe will bring you more of the same. This is where EFT can be used on a daily basis to keep you thinking positively even when life challenges get you down.

CHAPTER SIX

Tapping on Hidden Motives

Tapping on The Essence.

Ok, so let's dive right back into the story. In the last section you began to develop your new story. You also found the essence of why you want what you want. We'll begin tapping on the essence issues because these underlie your desire.

If you want something or even someone because you believe that it or they will make you feel a certain way then it's the feeling you're looking for. That means that you're currently experiencing a lack of that feeling in your life right now. Otherwise, you wouldn't be looking for it outside of yourself.

In my example, I wanted a successful business, but underneath that was a motivation to prove myself. Now, I might also want a successful business for many reasons, but if my feeling of self-worth isn't strong, then my business will most likely either fail or not do as well as I would like.

It doesn't matter what the positive reasons are. I also want to help people and make a difference in people's lives. I know the benefits of tapping and manifestation and so I want to share that with others. However, I can do that with or without a business.

If I'm unconsciously focused on proving myself then I'm sending a message to the universe that I'm unworthy. When I look at my reflection in the mirror, I'm seeing unworthiness reflected back to me because that is what I'm giving out. Does that make sense?

When we are dealing with issues regarding self-worth we're usually dealing with the belief that we don't deserve something. Now, I don't know what your essence desire is but I know that the most common ones that I hear are always the beliefs that, "I don't deserve to be wealthy, successful or to receive love."

These beliefs often stem from our childhood experiences of being criticised, judged and in some cases abused. It might not come directly from having been told we didn't deserve something either. We may have mirrored someone in our family who believed they didn't deserve wealth, success or love.

In this next tapping activity, you will be using your own dot points from the previous exercise in the last section. I hope you've written them down. Just substitute them for the blank lines in the script below. You can also add other statements if they feel right to you as you are tapping.

I'll give you an example below of how to substitute your own feelings and goals in the *basic recipe* statement. Then do the same for all of the tapping points.

These were my dot points:

totally free

do what I most enjoy

use my skills and talents
actualise my potential
self-worth

I'm going to tap on one of them at a time. So, I'll choose self-worth or worthiness.

Karate Chop: Even though I believe that I must achieve my goal of having a successful business in order to feel worthy, I deeply and completely accept myself.

Karate Chop: Even though I feel that the only way to feel worthy is to have a successful business, I honour how I feel.

Karate Chop: Even though I really believe that I don't deserve success, I choose to honour this and I am working toward changing this limiting belief.

Eyebrow point: I really want to have a successful business

Side of the Eye: If I achieve success then I'll finally feel worthy.

Under the Eye: I feel like I have to have to be successful in order to be worthy in the eyes of my family.

Under the Nose: But I don't feel worthy enough to have that success.

Above the Chin: I feel I don't deserve it.

Collarbone: I feel like someone is telling me that I don't deserve it.

Under the Arm: I feel like my family are telling me that I don't deserve it.

So now it's your turn.

Just be aware that even though scripts are very good guidelines, they can't substitute completely for a skilled practitioner.

As you are tapping there may be other beliefs or realisations that come up for you. You can make a note of these and tap on them too. You may even add them to the script once you get used to the process of tapping.

Let's Tap

You already know all about the basic recipe and the karate chop point, so let's dive right into the next activity.

Activity 13

Think about your essence desire and rate how true it feels on the 0 to 10 scale. Remember 0 is not true and 10 is very true.

Start tapping on the karate chop point and say the following:

Karate Chop: Even though, I believe that if I achieve my goal of .... I will feel ...., I deeply and completely accept myself.

Karate Chop: Even though I feel that the only way to feel .... is to have ...., I honour how I feel.

Karate Chop: Even though I really believe I don't deserve ...., I choose to honour this and I am working toward changing this limiting belief.

Eyebrow point: I really want to have ....

Side of the Eye: If I achieve .... then I'll finally feel ....

Under the Eye: I feel like I have to .... in order to be .... in .... eyes.

Under the Nose: But I don't feel .... enough to have that ....

Above the Chin: I feel I don't deserve it.

Collarbone: I feel like someone is telling me that I don't deserve it.

Under the Arm: I feel that my .... is telling me that I don't deserve it.

Eyebrow point: I really feel that I don't deserve to have that ....

Side of the Eye: What will happen if I achieve ....

Under the Eye: What will my .... say to me if I achieve ....

Under the Nose: How will my friends and family react if I achieve ....

Above the Chin: I feel I don't deserve it.

Collarbone: I feel like someone is telling me that I don't deserve it.

Under the Arm: I just can't imagine feeling any other way.

Eyebrow point: But what if there is another way to feel?

Side of the Eye: What if I can change this belief and this feeling of ....

Under the Eye: What if I do deserve to .... and feel ....?

Under the Nose: Oh, that feels weird!

Above the Chin: I'm just going to honour how I feel right now.

Collarbone: I'm just going to take one step at a time.

Under the Arm: I'm going to work on my willingness to change this belief.

Eyebrow point: Why don't I deserve ....?

Side of the Eye: In all reality, why don't I deserve to have ....?

Under the Eye: What if I do deserve to have .... and feel ....?

Under the Nose: What if I've been lying to myself all these years?

Above the Chin: About not being .... enough.

Collarbone: What if I am .... enough.

Under the Arm: How willing am I to change these old beliefs?

Eyebrow point: I'm beginning to want to really change this belief.

Side of the Eye: There's no good reason why I have to feel .... anymore.

Under the Eye: I can have .... without it proving that I'm ....

Under the Nose: I'm going to decide to be willing to deserve.

Above the Chin: Even if I've done things wrong in the past.

Collarbone: I choose to forgive myself.

Under the Arm: I'm looking forward to changing this old belief.

Take a deep breath and check in on the 0 to 10 scale to rate how you feel and how true your belief is. If it's still above a 3 go back and tap through those five rounds again. If you've hit 3 or less you can progress to the positive tapping sequence.

Eyebrow point: That's right, I'm just running an old program.

Side of the Eye: And programs can be changed.

Under the Eye: I choose to release the belief that I'm ....

Under the Nose: It's about time I changed it.

Above the Chin: It's about time I stop telling me that I'm ....

Collarbone: I'm just going to honour myself and how I feel right now.

Under the Arm: I'm going to work toward changing this limiting belief.

Eyebrow point: What if I do change this limiting belief that I'm....................

Side of the Eye: What if I do deserve ....

Under the Eye: I'm willing to believe it's possible.

Under the Nose: I'm willing to believe that I am ....

Above the Chin: I'm willing to believe that I have ....

Collarbone: I'm just going to honour that willingness.

Under the Arm: I'm going to see this as an opportunity to change my relationship with me.

Eyebrow point: I choose to have faith.

Side of the Eye: That I can step up and follow my goal of ....

Under the Eye: without it proving that I'm ....

Under the Nose: Because I'm choosing to believe that I am .... already.

Above the Chin: I'm choosing to believe that I have what it takes to be ....

Collarbone: Even if I'm not perfect at it all of the time.

Under the Arm: I'm choosing to believe in me and know that I am ....

Take a deep breath and check in with yourself again. Where are you on the 0 to 10 scale? If you're still above a 1 do the rounds again. If you're 1 or under then you must be feeling so much better right now.

Once you've got the limiting essence of what you want out of the way you can revisit what it is that you want and re-evaluate it. You may find that it's not so urgent anymore or that you aren't interested in having it anymore. That's ok. In fact, if it's not so pressing, then you have a much better chance of attracting it to you.

Once you've tapped on the limiting belief behind your desire, you'll find that the positive essence of what you want may feel stronger. It may have something to do with realising your potential and acting on it. If that comes through then you've done some really great work.

CHAPTER SEVEN

Tapping Away the Layers

The Magic Wand

So now I'm going to come along with my magic wand (yes, I really do have one) and say to you that you can have anything you want.

Imagine, a fairy godmother. We all imagined that as children. There are so many stories of magical fairies, genii and wishing wells, so why not use these to our advantage.

Let's say that I have my magic wand and I'm going to guarantee that what you've written down in your story will surely happen.

How do you feel about that?

In the next activity I want you to rewrite your story as if it has **ALREADY** happened. That's right! It's **ALREADY** happened. Right now, it's happened.

Write your story "as if" the experiences are in the present. It's happening to you now. You have what you want.

Activity 14

Write down your story as if it's happening right now.

Read the story as you write it down. The more senses you involve in your desire the more energy you are putting into it.

Try and write at least one whole page or more. I want lots of detail. The more detail you add, the more involved you'll get. The more involved you get, the more the limiting beliefs will start to show themselves.

Speak, write and visualise your perfect life.

How Does It Feel?

Once you've written everything down, spoken it out loud and visualised it, I want you to really sense how you feel about it. Now, this is an exercise in getting in touch with how you really feel about your dream life. Don't pretend to be all positive about it if you aren't. You'll have plenty of time for that later.

Read each desire in your dream out loud to yourself and write down how believable it is for you now. You can use the 0 to 10 scale, where 0 is unbelievable and 10 is believable.

I want you to also write down what thoughts or feelings are associated with that desire. Pay attention to that inner whispering. Try to catch the negative internal dialogue and write it down. Give that internal dialogue a score between 0 and 10 as well.

For example, you might have the following sentence in your story:

"I want to earn $100 000 dollars a year doing what I love."

I might rate the believability as a 7 and my internal dialogue might be saying, "You could never earn $100

000 a year doing that. Who do you think you are? How are you going to achieve that?"

The Universe is hearing: never earn $100 000 doing what you love; unworthy; unachievable.

The limiting thoughts that come for you when you are living your desire in your mind are called tailenders.

We experience these when we do affirmations as well. They are our subconscious programs playing a response to our conscious mind's attempt to think differently.

The tailenders are the heckling voices we hear after we state a positive affirmation and they negate our ability to carry out the statement. They are subconscious whispers telling you that you can't really achieve that, or you don't have what it takes etc.

These tailenders are so subtle that we often don't know we have them. It's the tailenders that the universe is hearing because the subconscious mind is playing them.

It doesn't matter how many times the conscious mind says a positive affirmation, if there is incongruence between it and your subconscious mind not much can happen.

If you spend the time doing this exercise, you'll have a very good understanding of where your subconscious thoughts are at the present time. You'll also have a good understanding of what the universe is hearing.

Don't panic. We'll fix this soon, but for now we need to see all of the dirt before we clean up the mess.

Sphere of Believability

Some of your goals may seem quite unbelievable to

you right now. They may be so different to anything you've already experienced that you just CAN'T see yourself experiencing them without a lot of heckling from your inner critic.

The best way to deal with this is to break the desire down to something closer to what you perceive to be more possible. For example: if you're earning $50K a year and you want to earn $1 million, that might be really hard to imagine let alone believe.

In this case the best thing to do is to focus on doubling your current income to $100 000 instead. Now even $100 000 will seem unbelievable but not as unbelievable a $1 million.

It's important to push your boundaries and go in a zone that's uncomfortable, however, it's best to do it in stages.

As you start tapping you will be able to increase the goal because your resistance will lessen. So, after tapping on $100 000 a year for awhile you might find it easier to tap on $250 000 a year and eventually get to that $1 million, if that is your goal.

So, let's look at tapping away those tailenders that are coming from your inner critic.

Tapping Away the Tailenders

In the next activity you're going to be tapping on the limiting beliefs you collected from the previous activity. These are your tailenders.

I'm going to give you an example of how you can use tapping to release those tailenders. For this example, I am going to use the ones from the previous activity.

They were the tailenders that came out of the desire to earn $100 000 a year doing what you love.

You could never earn $100 000 doing what you love.

Who do you think you are?

What will people say if you earned that much money?

How are you going to do that?

Go back to the list of limiting beliefs in chapter 2 and see if any of them have shown up somewhere in your tailender comments.

When I look closely at the above points, I see that a common theme here are feelings of unworthiness and a general underlying feeling of not really deserving the kind of lifestyle that you want.

In the next activity I'm going to lead you through a tapping sequence that's based on a common limited belief which is: "I don't deserve to have the lifestyle I want." I'll use the points above throughout the sequence as an example of how it all works.

A lot of people have the belief that they aren't worthy of their dream career, loving relationship or purpose in life. The feeling of deserving goes way back into childhood and can greatly affect how successful you become in your life.

Removing the beliefs around not deserving or being unworthy can free you up considerably so that you can start to express your full potential. It can also help you find your life purpose.

You most likely knew what your purpose was when you were a child but it became oppressed because you couldn't express that side of yourself. Maybe it wasn't safe to express your true self. Perhaps your true nature just didn't please the adults around you.

When that happens, we bury our needs and desires away. They're buried so deeply that we forget they even exist.

So, let's start tapping.

Activity 15

You know the drill. Rate how strong you feel the feeling of not deserving or being unworthy of the life you want on the 0 to 10 scale.

Add any thoughts and feelings to the script that feel right to you. You don't have to follow these scripts verbatim. They are just general scripts that are made up of the thoughts and feelings I hear the most from people.

As this is a general script please add more specific goals and dreams where appropriate. The more specific you are the better. If $100 000 is just way too much for you to imagine or if you don't have a monetary goal, just substitute what works for you.

Karate Chop: Even though I believe that I don't deserve that kind of lifestyle, I am working on changing my thinking about it.

Karate Chop: Even though I think that I'm not worthy enough to earn $100 000 a year doing what I love, I accept how I think and feel encouraged that I can change this.

Karate Chop: Even though I believe that I am not worthy and that my desire to have that happy and abundant lifestyle just isn't possible. I'm going to accept how I feel anyway.

Eyebrow point: I don't deserve that kind of life.

Side of the Eye: Who do I think I am?

Under the Eye: This could never happen to me.

Under the Nose: It's impossible.

Above the Chin: How would people react?

Collarbone: No, I just don't deserve it.

Under the Arm: How could I earn that much doing what I love?

Eyebrow point: People would be angry with me.

Side of the Eye: They'd hate me.

Under the Eye: And I have to keep everyone else happy.

Under the Nose: It's all about keeping others happy.

Above the Chin: I certainly don't deserve that kind of happiness.

Collarbone: No, I just don't deserve it.

Under the Arm: I'm better off just doing what I'm doing now.

Eyebrow point: How will I feel if I keep doing what I'm doing now?

Side of the Eye: Not that great actually.

Under the Eye: It would just be the same old thing.

Under the Nose: But at least I wouldn't be rocking the boat.

Above the Chin: I just don't deserve to earn that amount of money doing what I love?

Collarbone: No, I just don't deserve it.

Under the Arm: I'm better off just doing what I'm doing now.

Eyebrow point: Oh, I'm so over this!

Side of the Eye: I'm so over feeling like this.

Under the Eye: What if I can have that lifestyle?
Under the Nose: No, not me!
Above the Chin: How could I do that?
Collarbone: But I'm so over feeling like this!
Under the Arm: Why don't I deserve it?
Eyebrow point: Why do I think I'm so unworthy of earning a great income doing what I love?
Side of the Eye: Where did this come from?
Under the Eye: I don't need to feel this.
Under the Nose: There's no reason why I should be so unworthy of this.
Above the Chin: I'm over this feeling of unworthiness.
Collarbone: I'm just going to keep tapping until it goes away.
Under the Arm: I'm going to keep tapping until I realise that being unworthy is a lie.
Eyebrow point: It's a lie I keep telling myself.
Side of the Eye: Even though I may have been told this as a child.
Under the Eye: I'm telling myself this now.
Under the Nose: Time to change the program.
Above the Chin: I'm over this feeling of unworthiness.
Collarbone: I'm just going to keep tapping until it goes away.
Under the Arm: I'm going to keep tapping until I realise that being unworthy is a lie.

Once again, check in with yourself and rate how you feel on the 0 to 10 scale. If it's greater than a 1, keep tapping.

Use this process to tap on all of your limiting beliefs.

Forget the How

You may be finding that your inner critic is questioning and doubting how you can achieve what you want.

We spend a lot of the time worrying about how it's all going to happen. When we start questioning how it's all going to happen, we are getting in the way of the universe, which gets in the way of it happening.

We are not the ones who make it happen. The universe does that. We send out our intent and the universe makes it happen. It takes care of the HOW! The universe leads you there via your intuition and by lining up events that are in sync with your vibration. Sometimes that takes time.

Here's a short tapping sequence you can do to get over worrying about the HOW.

Fill in the blank lines with your own desire and feelings.

Activity 16

Rate your concerns and feelings on the 0 to 10 scale.

Karate Chop: Even though I have no idea how .... could ever happen to me. I am willing to get out of the way and let the universe take charge of it.

Karate Chop: Even though I'm finding it really difficult to let go of the HOW. I'm willing to give it a go.

Karate Chop: Even though I believe that there is no way .... could ever happen to me. I'm going to accept how I feel anyway.

Eyebrow point: I want............... but I don't know how it's going to happen.

Side of the Eye: It's such a huge jump to get from where I am now to ....

Under the Eye: It can't happen, No way!

Under the Nose: It's much too much of a stretch.

Above the Chin: Can't see how it's going to happen.

Collarbone: So much would have to change.

Under the Arm: No. Can't figure out the how.

Eyebrow point: Ok. So, I can't stop thinking about the how.

Side of the Eye: Even though the how isn't up to me.

Under the Eye: It's a big leap of faith.

Under the Nose: To trust an invisible universal force to take care of that for me.

Above the Chin: It just all seems far-fetched.

Collarbone: But I'm willing to give it a go.

Under the Arm: So, I'm just going to have to let go of the how.

Eyebrow point: The how isn't up to me.

Side of the Eye: I can't see the big picture.

Under the Eye: I can't see all of the possibilities like the universe can.

Under the Nose: I can't see all of the people and events that are aligning their intent with mine in order to make the how happen.

Above the Chin: I'm just a small drop in the ocean.

Collarbone: But I'm willing to give it a go.

Under the Arm: There are so many possibilities out

there that I don't know of.

Eyebrow point: Wow, I didn't realise how vast the possibilities are.

Side of the Eye: Anything can happen.

Under the Eye: I don't have a clue how it's going to happen.

Under the Nose: And maybe that's a good thing.

Above the Chin: I can just relax and let it happen.

Collarbone: All I have to do is follow my inner guidance.

Under the Arm: And the Universe will lead me there.

Eyebrow point: I think this is what people call faith.

Side of the Eye: I don't have to think about the how.

Under the Eye: The how doesn't belong to me.

Under the Nose: What a relief.

Above the Chin: I can just relax and let it happen.

Collarbone: All I have to do is follow my inner guidance.

Under the Arm: And the Universe will lead me there.

Once again, check in with yourself and rate how you feel on the 0 to 10 scale. If it's greater then a 1, keep tapping.

Now that you've tapped away the limiting beliefs, it's time to rewrite your story.

As you rewrite your story listen for other limiting beliefs and concerns about how it's all going to happen.

Releasing your limiting beliefs is like peeling an artichoke. You may find there are layers and layers that need to be peeled away. Keep peeling until you really feel like you believe your new story is possible.

We'll play some more with your story in part 4 but for

now keep tapping away those limiting beliefs.

In the next chapter, you'll begin to raise your present vibration so that your work toward magnetising what you want will be so much more powerful.

CHAPTER EIGHT

Focusing on The Now

Question Your Beliefs About Now

We're going to take a break away from thinking about what you want in the future and focus on what you have right now.

What you are thinking and feeling about where you are now, in your life, is crucial to how you will live your life in the future. This can be challenging for a lot of people. Especially if your life is far from what you want it to be right now.

I'll give you an example. I had a friend who was in a very difficult financial situation. Her business had failed and she was beside herself with worry about how she was going to keep the mortgage on her house. It seemed like she was going to lose everything she had. Every time I'd hear from her, things would be worse.

She believed in manifestation and thought she knew a lot about it. She tried many things but nothing was working. I could clearly see how she was blocking her success but as she was an "expert" she wouldn't listen.

You see, the problem was that she didn't really understand how the law of attraction really works. Sure, she knew how to visualise and channel energy toward her goals, but she didn't see any good in where she was in the present moment. All she talked about and focused upon was lack. So, lack was what she was sending out to the universe.

Now, even though her life was difficult, she still had some good things going for her. Yet, she felt that these things were so unimportant, when compared to her difficult money circumstances, that she refused to focus on them. Consequently, not much improved for her.

Manifesting what we want relies on us being in a very high positive vibration. This means that we have to be in a positive emotional and energetic state. If we are focused on what we don't have then we are focusing on lack and telling the universe to give us lack in return.

When you find yourself in a state where you are focused on what you don't have in your present moment, stop and start tapping. Tap on whatever it is that you are focused upon and bring it into your consciousness.

Once you bring it into conscious awareness, tap on it until it feels less intense and then start tapping on what you appreciate instead.

Focusing on what you do have in the present moment sends a message to the universe that you like what you have and so the universe will give you more of it. You will also attract a lot of other positive relationships and opportunities into your life as well. This is how you build positive momentum.

So, question the beliefs you have about how your life is now.

You might have a domineering boss. Maybe your co-workers are a pain to work with. Perhaps you are working long hours but not getting a lot of money in return. Maybe you have to travel a long way to work and back and you don't have enough time to spend with your family. That's all pretty negative stuff, right?

How can you turn that around to make it more positive? Well, you can use tapping for that.

Tapping on The Yuck of Now

Activity 17

Write a list of what you don't like about your "now".

Choose something on that list.

Now ask yourself the following questions:

What emotions do you feel most when you think about this situation?

What sensations do you feel in your body?

What thoughts do you have in relation to this situation?

I'll use the unfulfilled job scenario as an example but if that isn't your issue then substitute your own words instead.

The answers to the above questions might go like this:

Emotionally, I might feel bored, frustrated, angry and hopeless. I might feel tightness in my neck and shoulders. My thoughts might be, "I don't want to be here", "Is this all there is" and "I can't see a way out of this".

So now I'm going to rate these feelings, thoughts and sensations as a 7 on the 0 to 10 scale.

Karate Chop: Even though I feel frustrated, angry and

hopeless, I completely accept how I feel.

Karate Chop: Even though I'm thinking about how hopeless this job situation is, I'm choosing to do something about it now.

Karate Chop: Even though, I feel all of this tension in my neck and shoulders when I think about how hopeless my work situation seems, I accept myself and how I feel.

Eyebrow point: This hopelessness

Side of the Eye: All of this feeling of hopelessness about my job.

Under the Eye: I hate it so much.

Under the Nose: I'm so over it.

Above the Chin: All of this tension in my neck and shoulders

Collarbone: All of this anger and hopelessness in my neck and shoulders.

Under the Arm: I'm so frustrated about my job.

Eyebrow point: It's so boring!

Side of the Eye: I so hate my job.

Under the Eye: I'm so over working and not getting anything back.

Under the Nose: I'm so over it.

Above the Chin: It's all just too much.

Collarbone: How can I be positive when the situation feels so hopeless?

Under the Arm: How can I find anything to appreciate about this job?

Eyebrow point: It's so boring!

Side of the Eye: I so hate my job.

Under the Eye: I'm so over working and not getting anything back.

Under the Nose: I'm so over it.

Above the Chin: It's all just too much.

Collarbone: What can I find that's good about it?

Under the Arm: Is there anything good about it?

Eyebrow point: Surely there has to be something good about it.

Side of the Eye: Well, at least I have a job.

Under the Eye: It's serving an important purpose right now.

Under the Nose: I can pay the rent/mortgage.

Above the Chin: I can put food on the table.

Collarbone: It's letting me know what I don't want.

Under the Arm: And that has to be good for something.

Eyebrow point: Knowing what I don't want allows me to know what I do want.

Side of the Eye: So, I'm just going to find one good thing about this job.

Under the Eye: I only need to find one good thing and focus on that.

Under the Nose: Then I can begin to focus on what I do want without feeling all of those negative feelings about what I have.

Above the Chin: That one good thing is all I need to help me focus toward a higher vibration.

Collarbone: And that one good thing is that I have an income.

Under the Arm: And that income is serving me.

Eyebrow point: The income is serving me.

Side of the Eye: Even if it's not enough, it's better than nothing.

Under the Eye: And I'd like a higher income to serve me even more.

Under the Nose: So, I'm just going to honour how my job is serving me.

Above the Chin: I'm going to honour that while I focus on how it serves me that the universe will hear me and provide me with more income.

Collarbone: The universe will provide me with more choices and avenues of income.

Under the Arm: So, all I have to do is focus on how I have an income and how much I appreciate this.

Check in with the 0 to 10 scale again. If you're still above a 1 keep tapping and adding things. Really try to find some positive elements to where you are at the moment, so that you can increase what goes into your sphere of availability.

I know this stuff is icky and most law of attraction teachers have told you not to focus on what you don't want. But I'm sure you'll find that after tapping for half an hour or so, using the above method, that you'll experience a cognitive shift and begin to feel the vibrational connection between what you feel now and what can come to you.

The present and the future are linked. Your present determines your future. What you think and feel in the present opens the door to what becomes possible in your sphere of availability.

Sphere of Availability

Your sphere of availability contains the things that are ready to come into your life. Most things happen step by step. You'll find that larger dreams and goals often require smaller steps before they materialise. What comes to you must fit what you are ready for.

What comes into your sphere of availability are the things that you believe you can achieve and are able to receive. Each time you achieve something, more of it can filter into your sphere. Every time you let go of a limiting belief your sphere of availability expands to allow more of the things you want.

As the sphere widens, all of the situations, people and events that seemed not possible before can start flowing into your life. This is why it's so important to focus on the things you have already. It's also a good reason to celebrate every small step along the way to your goal. These small "wins" are like bread crumbs that lead the way to your major goal.

Now the sphere of availability works both ways. Things you don't want can enter into it if you're not watchful toward your beliefs and your perceptions.

There are many ways in which you can expand your sphere of availability to include more of what you want. I'll include some more activities to help you achieve that.

The Power of Appreciation

One of the most powerful ways that you can expand your sphere of availability is to practice the art of appreciation. Appreciation is different to gratitude.

Appreciation has a lighter feel to it. We usually use this word when we are acknowledging something we really enjoy. For example, I would say that I was appreciative of how easy it is to work alongside a particular person, say Peter. It has a very positive and uplifting feel to it.

Gratitude is often used in the same context as appreciation. However, it often denotes some level of comparison with something unwanted. For example, I might be grateful that I work with Peter instead of Dennis.

This is why I recommend you think in terms of appreciation. This will remove the risk of comparison between what you like verses what you don't like.

One of the common ways people use appreciation with law of attraction is to write down 10 things they appreciate about their day every day. I recommend that you start doing this as it allows you to see how even the little things can make a difference to your attitude.

The list can include simple things like the beautiful indigo colour of the sky at dusk or the soft and smooth feeling of your cat's fur brushing against your leg. These are the things we forget to appreciate and they can subtly increase your vibration.

So, do that right now. Write down 10 things you appreciate about your life. You can have more than 10 if you wish. Do this every day and see the difference it makes to your day and what you attract.

Tapping on Appreciation

You can power up your items of appreciation by tapping on them after you write them down. This reinforces them into your subconscious mind. I'll give you an example of some of the things that I am appreciating right now while I'm writing this book.

Eyebrow point: I really appreciate working from home.

Side of the Eye: I really love earning money doing what I love.

Under the Eye: I love the sound of the birds chirping through the silence.

Under the Nose: I really like the fact that I can look at the blue cloudless sky through my window.

Above the Chin: I'm really enjoying my cup of coffee.

Collarbone: I love how my cat comes in to visit me while I'm writing.

Under the Arm: I love the fact that it's a warm sunny day.

You can do this throughout your day to give yourself a reminder of the good things you have. I'd recommend doing it at least 3 times a day.

If you do this over the course of a month you should start to see some changes in the way you feel. The more often you practice appreciation, the more you will reinforce the habit of positive thinking into your subconscious mind.

Be Mindful of your B-B-Buts

"How can I be appreciative of my life when all of this bad stuff is happening to me?"

The truth is, if you're focusing on just the bad stuff, which most people do, then you're just going to continue to feel like crap. More importantly, you're probably not going to be attracting anything really helpful or better into your life while you are feeling so down.

A word of caution though! Many people think that if they want to practice positive manifestation that they have to be positive all of the time. That's not true.

It's natural to face difficult times and it's normal to react to them with the emotions of anger, grief and fear. These emotions are natural and we have them for a reason.

Emotions like anger, fear and grief let us know some pretty important information. We might be angry because we feel we are being victimised or we might feel fear because something is a threat to us.

We shouldn't try to suppress these feelings or even avoid them. We should just acknowledge that they are there, tap on them to release the blocked energy, gain clarity about the situation, and then act accordingly.

The important thing is that we don't become attached to our emotions. Having emotions is natural and necessary. The problem occurs when we become so attached to the feeling that we identify with it as if it's what we are.

We say things like, "I'm angry", or "I'm scared". We are not anger or fear. We feel anger and fear, and that is all. Anger and fear let us know that something is not quite right either within us or around us. We then have the choice to do something about ourselves or the situation we are in.

Our emotions are our guidance system. They let us know important things about where we are on the scale of vibration. They let us know where our energy is vibrating at. They are neither good nor bad.

Emotions just serve a function. It's really that simple. So don't beat yourself up about feeling uncomfortable emotions. Just see them as signs that some work needs to be done somewhere.

If we treat uncomfortable emotions as allies instead of foes, we can utilise them to help us grow as people and as powerful magnetic individuals.

Tapping on those Buts

If you're still having trouble finding things to appreciate in your life then tap on the BUTS. You will find that tapping on your objections to appreciating anything in your life will help you find things to appreciate.

We're going to do another tapping round on the BUTS. This will help you discover your own blocks that are getting in your way and preventing you from changing your circumstances.

I'm going to be general here and let you fill in the blanks with your own words. Try to be as detailed as you can. Like I've said before, the more detailed you can be the better.

Activity 18

Karate Chop: Even though everything seems so bad right now. I completely accept how I feel.

Karate Chop: Even though I don't see anything to appreciate in my life right now, I'm choosing to do something about it now.

Karate Chop: Even though, I feel like there is nothing important in my life right now that I want to appreciate, I accept myself and how I feel.

Eyebrow point: Things just seem so bad right now.

Side of the Eye: All of this feeling of hopelessness about this situation.

Under the Eye: How can I find something to appreciate.

Under the Nose: I'd rather just focus on what's going wrong in my life.

Above the Chin: It's easier to focus on what's not going right.

Collarbone: What difference will appreciating the blue sky do to help my situation?

Under the Arm: The whole exercise seems so futile.

Eyebrow point: But what if I just try to give it a go.

Side of the Eye: What if I can find just one thing to appreciate?

Under the Eye: Ok, I'll try to find one thing right now that I like.

Under the Nose: I'm trying to find something.

Above the Chin: It doesn't have to be a big thing.

Collarbone: Ok, I'm going to find something to appreciate.

Under the Arm: I appreciate ....

Eyebrow point: There I said it.

Side of the Eye: I've found one thing to appreciate.

Under the Eye: Maybe I can find something else to appreciate.

Under the Nose: I'm trying to find something.

Above the Chin: Ok, I appreciate...

Collarbone: Good, now I have two things.

Under the Arm: I'm just going to keep tapping on these

things.

Keep tapping on the things you appreciate. Play a game with yourself. Give yourself 1 minute to find as many things to appreciate in your life as you can.

How many things did you come up with?

Becoming a magnet to what you want does take work. It's not necessarily easy. The more self-aware you become, the more control you can take over your own life.

Let's Be Clear About Guilt and Selfishness

I know people who have trouble focusing on what they want. Many people have so much resistance inside of them that they avoid making the time to really sit down and focus on what they desire.

I've heard people say that they feel guilty when they try to think about what they want. Sometimes it just seems selfish to want so much when other people appear to be suffering so much more than we are.

If we want to enjoy our lives, we need to get over the guilt trip and get clear on what we do want. The law of attraction belief system includes the belief that the universe is an abundant place. That means that you are not denying some other person something by having it yourself.

It's a hard concept to get our head around because when we look at "reality" we think we see so much evidence of scarcity. It's seems selfish and harsh to say that people who are living in poverty simply have a scarcity mentality.

Many of these people don't have a scarcity mentality.

They just have different definition of wealth.

We have to understand that our idea of scarcity and wealth is based on our western lifestyle and culture. It's true that in our western culture we tend to focus on things. There are many cultures that hold family and community above material possessions.

We might look at people living in impoverished countries and see them as lacking, but I've heard so many stories from people from these countries who say how privileged they were to live in cultures that value family and community over possessions.

We must understand how cultures differ in values in order to understand how vast law of attraction is and just how abundance manifests for different people.

We don't really know what other people are experiencing inside of themselves or what their values are. All of these things determine what they attract into their lives.

Feeling guilty or selfish is a waste of time. It's not up to you what other people receive or don't receive. Even when you donate a blanket to a charity, it's still not up to you who receives it.

Having said all of that it is important for you to concentrate on manifesting what you are comfortable manifesting. Otherwise, you're just going to get in your own way.

So many people sabotage their success in finance, love and health because of feelings of shame around being selfish. It all comes down to choice. You can stay were you are and learn to live with it or you can learn to challenge your beliefs and design the life you want.

The next tapping activity focuses on releasing those feelings of guilt and selfishness associated with wanting what you want. I know this can be challenging to some people but please give it a go.

Activity 19

Karate Chop: Even though I feel guilty about having .... when other people are struggling. I completely accept myself and how I feel.

Karate Chop: Even though I feel selfish for wanting .... I honour how I feel.

Karate Chop: Even though, I believe that wanting .... is selfish and I feel guilty, I choose to love myself anyway and I'm just going to tap on this and see where it leads me.

Eyebrow point: I feel selfish.

Side of the Eye: I feel selfish for wanting .... while others are struggling.

Under the Eye: It all just seems so selfish.

Under the Nose: And it is selfish.

Above the Chin: Wanting something for myself is selfish.

Collarbone: I've been taught by so many people that it's wrong to be selfish. That it's wrong to want things for myself.

Under the Arm: I've been taught to feel guilty.

Eyebrow point: I don't want to seem selfish.

Side of the Eye: But I feel selfish.

Under the Eye: And I guess I am being selfish.

Under the Nose: Being selfish is about wanting things for myself.

Above the Chin: Wanting to feel good is being selfish.

Collarbone: I've been taught by so many people that it's wrong to be selfish. That it's wrong to want things for myself.

Under the Arm: Does that mean that it's wrong to want to feel good.

Eyebrow point: Does that mean that I should aim to feel bad because I assume others are feeling bad?

Side of the Eye: Does that mean that I should aim to have nothing because other people appear to having nothing?

Under the Eye: I've never questioned the concept of selfishness.

Under the Nose: I've just believed what I was told.

Above the Chin: That wanting something for myself was selfish.

Collarbone: I've been taught by so many people that it's wrong to be selfish. That it's wrong to want things for myself.

Under the Arm: I've never questioned this.

Eyebrow point: I've never questioned what selfishness really is.

Side of the Eye: I just feel guilty for believing that I am selfish for wanting to feel good.

Under the Eye: I don't like admitting that I'm selfish.

Under the Nose: But if I want something for myself and to feel good, then I am being selfish.

Above the Chin: Being selfish is about wanting for self.

Collarbone: I've been taught that this is somehow wrong.

Under the Arm: If I am selfish then someone else has to

suffer.

Eyebrow point: I'm starting to wonder if any of these makes sense.

Side of the Eye: Does my abundance really cause scarcity for someone else?

Under the Eye: I don't like admitting that I'm selfish.

Under the Nose: But if I want something for myself and to feel good, then I am being selfish.

Above the Chin: Maybe I need to review this notion of selfishness.

Collarbone: Maybe it's not so bad after all.

Under the Arm: Maybe it's all a misunderstanding.

Eyebrow point: I don't want other people to suffer.

Side of the Eye: But does my having really cause scarcity for someone else?

Under the Eye: If I have abundance then I am more able to share and give.

Under the Nose: I can't give what I don't have.

Above the Chin: Maybe I need to review this notion of selfishness.

Collarbone: I'm not trying to deprive other people. I just want to enjoy my life.

Under the Arm: I can't create for other people anyway.

Eyebrow point: How does my deprivation help other people anyway?

Side of the Eye: How does my lack help someone else's lack?

Under the Eye: How does my suffering help other people who are suffering?

Under the Nose: I can't give what I don't have.

Above the Chin: What if what we've been told about selfishness is not quite right?

Collarbone: What if it's ok to be selfish in some ways.

Under the Arm: I can't create for other people anyway.

We have been told that selfishness is wrong and selflessness is right. But that is very black and white thinking. I'm not proposing that we be selfish in a harmful way to others. What I am saying is that living a happy life with the people and things in it that give us pleasure and comfort aren't bad.

Remember, the universe is an abundant place and there is plenty of abundance to go around. We, however, are the only ones who can bring it into our lives.

PART FOUR

CREATE YOUR FUTURE

Now that you know how to work with the limiting beliefs through tapping you are ready to focus on what it is that you want and attract it all to you.

In previous chapters we've explored how the subconscious mind plays a major role in supporting our efforts to manifest what we want. We've also discussed how to find limiting beliefs and release them.

Now you're going to learn how to create and reinforce positive beliefs into your subconscious mind. You're going to start creating a new program.

These new programs will eventually replace the old limiting programs. As this happens you will find that the things you want will start to manifest at a faster rate.

There are a lot of methods that you can use to help put you into the right mindset to attract what you want. We're going to cover some of them in the next couple of chapters. You can use tapping alongside of these methods to enhance your power and focus.

Magnetising is about attracting. We know from earlier chapters that we are magnetic beings because our magnetism can be measured. We can enhance our magnetism by developing our inner selves.

Self-development is a creative process. Even though the universe makes it all happen, we still need to find creative ways to put ourselves into the right mindset to energetically communicate to the universe what it is that we want.

Only in the joyous and uplifted state can we attract what we want to ourselves. It's really all about us. The universe is just mirroring what we are energetically displaying.

CHAPTER NINE

Tapping into Abundance

Living the Story

We've done some pretty intensive work on releasing those limiting beliefs and now it's time to focus on bringing what you do want into your physical reality.

You may have had trouble finding what it is that you really want. Perhaps you have a vague idea but aren't very clear. Or you may have a detailed idea of how you want your future to look.

So just to recap a little. You find out what you do want by becoming aware of what you don't want.

So often when I ask people what they would like to create they will say things like, "I don't want to work in this crappy, soul destroying job anymore," or "I don't want to get up at 6 am in order to go to work." These are things they don't want. Focusing too much on what we don't want only brings us more of the same.

Having said that, we have to focus on what we don't want for a brief time in order to come up with an alternative.

I'm hoping that you know by now what you want even if it's only in a general way.

In previous chapters, you wrote a story about the life you'd like to have. Now that you've tapped on a few of the common blocks and resistance, it's time to work on the detail.

It's also possible that what you initially wanted has changed as you've worked on the hidden essence of what you wanted. That's ok. It's all about getting to know yourself better anyway.

You've also tapped on any resistance you have to being more appreciative about what you already have. If you've followed all of the activities in this book then you are ready to start really focusing on the life you really want.

So, let's get right back into it. This whole manifesting process is an active process. You can't manifest what you want simply by reading about how to do it. You actually need to **DO IT**!

Activity 20

Go back over your story and rewrite it in more detail. This time, while you're writing it, think about the person who is going to be living this life. That person is of course you.

Really, imagine you are this person.

How does it feel?

Do you feel like you are this person right now?

Do you feel like a match to the person and lifestyle?

One way to find out how it will feel to live the life you want is to think like an actor. Actors research their characters and then take on their characteristics. They Act "as if" they were that character.

What if you were to act "as if" you were that person in your story right now?

Try it out?

Visualise the "you" in that story.

How do you walk?

How do you talk?

What are you talking about?

Go on act it out. Find a secluded space and act out a scene from your story.

How does it feel?

Does it feel good?

Does it feel uncomfortable in any way when you imagine you are this person?

Do you feel like a fake?

Does this person in your story fit your current identity?

What would it take to feel like that person?

If you are waiting for your circumstances to change before you can feel like the person in your story then you may be waiting a long time. Remember, what you are feeling now influences what you'll get. So, if you really want that future then you need to start believing and feeling like that person now.

Don't worry, it doesn't need to happen overnight. It's like you're planting a seed and over time with care and attention the seed will grow into a tree.

If your future self just seems too way off who you are right now then you may need to tap on the discomfort. You may find there are hidden beliefs about your capabilities and worthiness.

You've had your current identity for most of your life so it's not something that is going to feel easy to change. However, just because it doesn't feel easy doesn't mean you can't change.

You are more than you think you are!

There are so many personality characteristics in you that you have never explored before. When you start removing your resistance through tapping, then you'll start to discover some of the personality characteristics which have been hidden.

We think that our personalities are limited to who we have grown up believing we are. In the world of magic and manifestation, what you can imagine, you can bring into reality. If you can imagine yourself a certain way, even if it feels uncomfortable, you can be that person. It might take some time but it can be done.

I'm going to include another tapping script for you that addresses the discomfort you may feel about your future self.

Activity 21

Remember to rate your belief and feelings on the 0 to 10 scale. Please feel free to substitute your own words and add you own thoughts where necessary.

Karate Chop: Even though I don't feel comfortable when I try to imagine myself as the person in my story, I deeply and completely accept myself.

Karate Chop: Even though I really want to be……………… and have ……………, acting it out makes me feel like a fake, but I'm willing to change the way I feel about myself and my identity.

Karate Chop: Even though I feel awkward imagining myself as that person with all of those things in my life, I know that I can change this and trust that I can express those qualities.

Eyebrow point: I feel like a fake.

Side of the Eye: How can I be like that?

Under the Eye: I can't imagine myself being that person.

Under the Nose: It just feels uncomfortable.

Above the Chin: It feels weird.

Collarbone: Can I really be the kind of person who can have that lifestyle?

Under the Arm: I'm not like that.

Eyebrow point: If I became like that then my identity would change.

Side of the Eye: I won't feel like me.

Under the Eye: And this makes me feel uncomfortable.

Under the Nose: I don't feel like that person can exist inside of me.

Above the Chin: I'm not used to being that kind of person

Collarbone: I'm not used to showing that side of my personality.

Under the Arm: Maybe I've never really allowed myself to explore that part of my personality.

Eyebrow point: It feels like I have to change my identity.

Side of the Eye: And that feels uncomfortable.

Under the Eye: I'm just going to honour that discomfort.

Under the Nose: I'm going to just sit with that feeling.

Above the Chin: I don't have to change myself in any way.

Collarbone: I just need to grow that part of me.

Under the Arm: It's a me that I haven't explored yet, that's all.

Eyebrow point: But I'll still be me.

Side of the Eye: I'll just be an enhanced me.

Under the Eye: I'll just be a larger version of me.

Under the Nose: I'll be adding to my personality.

Above the Chin: I'll still be me.

Collarbone: I'm going to allow myself to expand.

Under the Arm: And if there are other reasons why I feel uncomfortable, I'll tap on them.

Now take a nice deep breath and relax. Check in with yourself and see how you are feeling. Use the scale from 0 to 10 to see if your feelings have changed.

Challenge all of the reasons why you can't be the person you would like to be. Most of these reasons aren't true, they are only beliefs you picked up from other people throughout your life.

The wonderful thing about learning to be a designer of your life is that you MUST learn about yourself and challenge yourself. It can't be done any other way.

Who you feel yourself to be now is causing you to have your current life. If your current life is all you want then don't change anything. The fact that you are reading this indicates that you'd like to make some changes.

Turning Up the Volume

Once you have tapped away your resistance you can

start to make your story more powerful by making your vision brighter and boost the positive emotional feelings in it.

You're going to do two things. First, you're going to use association. This is where you imagine yourself in the story as if you are experiencing it now.

The second thing you're going to do is play the story, like a move, with you as an observer. It will be like you are watching a movie with you in it. This is called disassociation.

Using both association and disassociation when visualising what you want adds power to your vision.

You're also going to use colour, brightness and distance to find which view of your movie is the most powerful one for you to use.

Activity 22

So, let's start with association. Close your eyes and imagine that you're in your story. Take notice of the colours in your story. Run the story and make the colours brighter.

Did you notice any difference in how it felt?

Run you story again and this time make it dull in colour.

Now how did that feel?

Experiment with the colour and brightness to find the level that makes you feel your best.

Changing the colour and brightness of your visualisation gives it a stronger feeling which influences your subconscious mind so that it thinks the visualisation is real.

This can be used every time you use visualisation to

manifest what it is that you want.

In the next activity we'll focus on the use of distance to help enhance the emotional effect.

Activity 23

Close your eyes and visualise your story again. This time, however, stand outside of the story as if you are in a movie theatre watching a movie.

Watch yourself in your story as you live your ideal life.

Now adjust the colour in the movie, make it brighter and then make it dull.

Experiment and see which one makes you feel better about the movie. Imagine the movie moves closer to you. Observe it for a few seconds and then move it further away.

Which one feels better, close up or further away?

When you imagine yourself in any of your ideal visualisations always experiment with the colour, brightness and distance. I'm sure you can feel the difference it makes by doing the last two activities.

These seemingly minor adjustments make a huge difference to the feel of the story. They'll also influence the message you're giving to the universe. This is because you'll be associating good feelings with the images and therefore the desire itself.

Bringing It into The Now

Now it's time to start acting as if you have what you want. If this still feels uncomfortable then keep tapping on those opposing thoughts and feelings. It might sound ridiculous to ask you to act as if you have what you want when you don't yet have it.

Children are very good at this. Remember when you were a child and you imagined being a warrior, celebrity or royalty. You weren't really a prince or princess but you could probably really get into the role. The only difference was that as a child you knew that you were playing "make believe".

Now as an adult you are playing for real. As an adult you can turn "make believe" into "make real".

If you're having strong resistance to this idea then go back to the previous tapping activity and add your current objections. It's only natural that this will feel strange.

It doesn't matter if you feel like a fake at first. It's supposed to feel that way. This is just resistance and it's how we learn.

We learn to be who we are by imitating other people so this isn't really any different. If we want to change our subconscious mind then we have to use imitation on a regular basis in order to rewrite the programs.

Here are some examples of how you can imitate the future you. For example, if the future you is driving your dream car and you currently drive a beat up old wreck, then every time you drive your current car, just imagine you're driving your dream car.

Sit in that car as you would your ideal car. Talk to it as if it is your ideal car. Treat it as if it's your ideal car. See your ideal car and appreciate it. Appreciate how it looks and feels. As you think, so you create. That's how it's done. Even if it seems ridiculous give it a go. What have you got to lose?

I'll give you some more activities that you can do to increase your "make real" experience.

If you want a relationship then pretend you already have one with the perfect person. Take yourself out to lunch or dinner. Imagine you are with that perfect person.

If you want a particular job or career, imagine you're already doing it. Even if you are currently in a job in which you do totally different activities, you can use your creative imagination and feel your way there.

You can do the same kinds of imaginary games for most situations. Just imagine yourself doing it even when you aren't. Remember, your subconscious mind can't tell the difference between what is real and what is imagined.

If you do the "make real" game enough, your subconscious mind will believe its real and lead you toward making it a reality.

Once you convince your subconscious mind that it's real, you are on your way to making it happen. That's how you magnetise what you want.

Give It All You've Got

We have amazing imaginations. Many of us tend to favour a particular sense over the others. Some people are very visual while others are very tactile. It's important to use as many of our senses as we can when we are working toward manifesting what we want. The more senses we use, the more real it becomes to our subconscious mind.

It's a little bit like living in a fantasy land where we are "pretending" that we are somewhere we're not. What we're trying to do is create another reality. This reality is one where we are living to our full potential and making a difference in the world in a way that fulfils our deepest needs.

We use our five senses to experience the material world. Many things can be experienced through all of our senses at once.

When we get into a new car, we can use our five senses to fully experience the car. We can smell the new upholstery. We can see the bright colour. The engine has a particular sound and the seats have a texture that we can touch. We could even taste it if we wanted to.

Activity 24

In this activity, I want you to observe what you can see, hear, touch, smell and, if appropriate, even taste right now. Just spend one minute observing as much as you can with at least four of your senses.

What does the seat you're sitting on feel like?

Can you smell anything?

What sounds can you hear?

What can you see around you?

Now narrow your focus to one object in particular.

What does it feel like?

Does it have a smell?

Does it give off a sound?

What does it look like?

Take note of the answers to these questions and then

close your eyes.

Can you bring back the sound, vision, smell and feeling of that object in your imagination?

Don't worry if you can't use all of your senses in this way. It's a skill that many people have to learn over time. Most people are good visualisers but others can't visualise at all. Yet they can recall a face or a place. It's all a matter of practise.

You can take each sense from the previous activity and practise with it. For example: Look at the object with your eyes open and really notice as much as you can about it. Close your eyes and see if you can bring back a picture of it in your mind's eye. Just practise doing that for 5 minutes every day until you can visualise the object without having to look at it first.

Some people don't understand what visualising really is. It isn't a matter of closing your eyes and seeing something there. If you're like most people you'll most likely only see black or some colours. That's not what we mean by visualise.

Visualising is seeing something in your imagination. It's the same method you use to remember a person's face when they're not there. If I said to you, "Do you know what your best friend looks like?" You'd probably have a picture of your friend in your imagination. It's just like that.

Once you've mastered the art of visualising you can do the same exercise with the other four senses. It goes like this:

Activity 25

To develop your auditory sense, grab a spoon and hit it against a glass. Do that a few times and then try to recall that sound in your imagination.

Touch something with your fingertips and feel its texture. Then use your imagination to recall the feeling with your fingertips. Continue this with taste and smell. Soon you'll be able to bring to mind anything you want and imagine how it looks, feels, sounds, smells and tastes, all in your imagination.

Let's go back to your story about your ideal life. Pick a scene in the story and imagine yourself in that scene.

What can you hear?

What do you see?

What can you smell?

What can you touch?

Is there any taste involved?

Make sure you can persist with this imagery for at least one minute. Master magicians practise the art of imagining every day in order to develop their skills to a high level.

If you really want to test yourself, do your imagination exercises with your eyes open. This is when you can start to see the changes around you even when they aren't physically there.

When you practice the sensory imagination skills in the activities above you will find that you'll be able to "make real" so much easier. When you live your story, you'll have your senses working for you and this will reinforce the believability in your subconscious mind.

You may even find that people will react differently to you and your perceptions of your current life will begin to change. Once your perceptions change so will your life.

Using Tapping to Enhance the story

As we now know, tapping calms the amygdala in the brain and can create a sense of calm. This calming feeling is positive and feeling positive increases our ability to manifest what we want.

You can use tapping to enhance your story.

Pick a feeling, belief or quality that you are going to need to manifest your story. For example, you may need to manifest the feeling of deserving in order to really feel joy in your story.

Craft an affirmation around this feeling, belief or quality. When crafting an affirmation make it in the present tense and make it positive.

Use words such as "I am" or "I feel" instead of "I will" or "I want". "I am" is in the present tense, whereas, "I will" is referring to something in the future. "I want" is focusing on what you want but don't have.

You should aim to affirm the feeling of already having what you want in the present moment. The reason why you must use the present tense because that's where you always are. You are always in the "Now".

I'll give you some examples of affirmations that focus on the feeling of deserving. I've chosen deserving because it is by far the most common block to manifesting what we want.

I deserve to have a successful business.

I am so appreciative and joyful about my beautiful house by the ocean.

I am worthy of having a fulfilling and loving relationship.

I enjoy helping people and earning a great income.

I deserve and enjoy a life of security and abundance.

I deserve to realise my potential and make a difference in the world.

You can also use, "I have, I know and I love".

Make up the affirmations from your story. Be creative and enjoy the process. The more fun you have with this the better.

Please don't ever treat any of your manifestation activities as chores, even the ones that focus on removing your blocks. This is all about expanding your awareness and sense of self, so it's a very positive and life affirming activity.

Write the affirmations in the style that you would say them. It's easy to find ready-made affirmations but the ones that are in your own words and resonate with your story will have more powerful results. Most importantly, write your affirmations with joyful feeling and passion.

There are a couple of ways that you can use tapping with your affirmations. If you just want to focus on one thing then you can do five minutes of tapping on all of the points while you say that one affirmation.

Alternatively, if you want to tap on a number of affirmations that align with your story then you can compile about eight of them and assign one to each tapping point. Do the tapping sequence 10 times.

Once you've worked out what kind of sequence you want to use commit to doing it every day for at least 21 days. It takes 21 days to create a habit and cement something into your subconscious mind.

While you are tapping focus on the positive emotions that you want to feel as you tap. Remember, emotion is where the energy is. The better you feel the stronger the magnetism.

Tap on It Until You Know It

Even though it only takes 21 days, don't stop tapping on something until you really feel like you believe it can come true. If you are tapping on deserving a loving relationship then don't stop tapping until you really feel like you deserve a loving relationship.

A Hypnotherapy Trick

If you want to use the power of social proof you can change your "I" statements into "You" statements. We are social animals and research has shown that messages are more believable to us when they are delivered by someone else.

So, who can that someone else be? Well it is you.

All you need to do is imagine that you have a doppelganger sitting in front of you and that they are saying those affirmations to you. This will demand that you have developed your sensory imagination skills to a high level but it's worth the time. It's a very powerful way to reinforce new beliefs into your subconscious mind.

There are many ways to reprogram the subconscious mind. The wonderful thing about the methods outlined in this program is that they only require yourself and some time.

CHAPTER TEN

Getting Out of The Way

The Art of Surrendering

I've already talked about the importance of not becoming too concerned about how your desires are going to manifest. That isn't up to you.

You can't possibly know all of possibilities out there. There are so many different ways that people and situations can synchronise with each. Often these events line up in ways that you could never have thought possible.

Not worrying about "the how" is how we get out of the way of our manifestation. That doesn't mean that we don't fantasise about the how, we just don't become obsessed with it.

In my experience, my manifestations never occur the way I thought they might. You see, so many things have to be aligned in order for people and events to line up with each other.

If you're to attract the right person into your life, whether that is a lover or simply someone to help you with something then both of you have to be in alignment with your intention.

So, the key here is to surrender to the universal force,

whatever that means to you or whatever name you may give it. Many religions and mystical traditions speak of surrendering to a higher power or divinity.

We are active and passive all at once when we deliberately set forth our desires. We are active in our thinking and feeling and passive in our letting go and receiving.

Mutual Alignment

Throughout history people have been concerned about negative implications associated with the manifestation of their desire.

"What happens if I put an intention out to gain money and my uncle dies and leaves me an inheritance? Am I responsible for his death?" These are very common questions.

In fact, these questions are so common, I hear them all of the time. Fortunately, it's not how it works.

In order for two events to align they have to be a vibrational match. That means that both people who meet and fall love have to be energetically available for this to happen.

Remember, our intentions are on the conscious and subconscious levels. Someone may not be consciously intending to fall in love but in order to do so they need to be open to it on some level.

It's the same with inheritances. The desire for money and the death of a relative who bequeaths you some money have to be in alignment before it can happen. You can't cause another person's death by wanting something. They have to be in that place where they are aligned with it. This comes from them, not you.

This is the same for influencing other people in general.

There is no law of assertion. You can't assert your intentions on to someone else. You can influence them but they have to be in a vibrational state that aligns with your influence. This state is influenced by their own beliefs about themselves and the world around them.

People were always scared of magic in the past because they believed that someone could harm them with magic.

If someone believes that they can be harmed then their subconscious mind will make it so. Scientists call it the nocebo effect and by definition it is the negative effect of a psychological belief that something is harmful, usually to health.

The expectations of harm cause the expression of that harm to manifest symptoms in a person who believes they are being harmed.

The same is true of the placebo effect but in reverse.

Everything has to align energetically. That's why it can take some time for some desires to manifest. You have to be in alignment with the people and events that are involved in the manifestation of your desire.

All of this alignment is out of your hands which makes working consciously with the law of attraction a matter of learning to surrender to a greater power.

Distract Yourself

In the next chapter you're going to learn some creative ways to help you make law of attraction even more fun but first you need to know some rules of the game.

The more you focus on what you want the more chance you have of getting it. However, you need to focus in a positive way. That means that you physically do what is necessary to bring the goal into reality and are living appreciatively in the present.

You must focus on the happy, joyful and fun aspects of bringing the goal into reality and not on the desperation for it to work.

One of the ways that you can get of the way of the universe is to find something else to focus on.

If being focused joyfully on your goal isn't possible then it is best to distract yourself away from thinking about it at all. Otherwise, you're just getting in the way of its manifestation.

Why Having to Have It or Else Causes Failure

Another way that you can sabotage your desire is to be desperate about the need for it to manifest. This is called lusting after the result. This need comes from the fear of not having it which is only projecting more fear to your subconscious mind and the universe.

That's why it's necessary to tap on all of the emotions associated with your goal. Let's do some tapping on this desperation so that it doesn't get in your way.

Activity 26

Rate how desperate you feel on the 0 to 10 scale and do the following sequence substituting your own feelings and beliefs where appropriate.

Karate Chop: Even though I really feel that I need for this

.... to happen, I deeply and completely accept myself.

Karate Chop: Even though I don't know what I'll do if .... doesn't manifest, I accept how desperate I feel.

Karate Chop: Even though I believe that if .... doesn't happen then I'll feel .... I'm just going to tap on this because I don't like this feeling of desperation.

Eyebrow point: I don't know what I'll do if............ doesn't happen.

Side of the Eye: I really need it to happen.

Under the Eye: I can't imagine what I'll do if things don't change.

Under the Nose: I don't know how to change this feeling.

Above the Chin: I just have to make this happen.

Collarbone: I just have to have ....

Under the Arm: I just feel so desperate about............

Eyebrow point: I don't know what I'll do if............ doesn't happen.

Side of the Eye: It's just got to happen.

Under the Eye: I don't want things to stay the same.

Under the Nose: But I feel so desperate.

Above the Chin: I feel so afraid of what life will be like if I don't get ....

Collarbone: If I don't get .... it will mean............

Under the Arm: I don't want to be in the same situation

I'm in now for the rest of my life.

Eyebrow point: All of this worry about it not happening.

Side of the Eye: I'm really trying to be positive about this.

Under the Eye: But I'm scared of what will happen if I don't get ....

Under the Nose: But I don't want to get in the universe's way.

Above the Chin: I don't want to want this so much.

Collarbone: I just wish I could change this wanting.

Under the Arm: I just wish I could lessen the feeling of fear and desperation.

Eyebrow point: Why can't I just relax and trust the universe?

Side of the Eye: Why can't I just trust myself a bit more?

Under the Eye: What if I just tap on this desperation every day?

Under the Nose: I'm trying to do something about it all.

Above the Chin: I can find a way to trust.

Collarbone: If I don't trust then why am I even doing this tapping?

Under the Arm: I must believe in this stuff to some extent.

Eyebrow point: What if I imagine what it would feel like to trust the universe?

Side of the Eye: And what it would feel like to be a powerful magnet to success.

Under the Eye: Other people manage to do it.

Under the Nose: I'm just going to allow myself to feel,

for just a minute, what this kind of power would feel like.

Above the Chin: So many other people have succeeded with law of attraction.

Collarbone: I can be one of them.

Under the Arm: Maybe this can happen without me worrying about it.

Eyebrow point: I'm just going to tap on this for a while until I feel more trust.

Side of the Eye: I want this to happen.

Under the Eye: I am willing to trust more.

Under the Nose: I'm willing to give this trust thing a go.

Above the Chin: It certainly will feel better to let go and trust.

Collarbone: So I'll just keep tapping until it happens.

Under the Arm: I'm going to keep tapping until I get out of my own way.

Rate how you're feeling on the 0 to 10 scale and keep tapping regularly on this subject until the feelings go down to at a 1.

Trust is a difficult thing to acquire and in the next chapter I will show you how you can develop trust in the law of attraction by practising small things on a regular basis.

Joy and The Emotional Scale

The whole point of doing all of this tapping is to remove all of those emotions that make you uncomfortable and exacerbate the limited thinking. The goal is for you to be able to function throughout your life in a more joyful and happier way.

The more joy we can experience the more joy we can attract into our lives. Joy is emotion and emotion is the energy which gives our magnetism greater power because it affects our energy signature.

Every emotion you feel affects your vibration which affects what you project outwardly. The universe will mirror this projection.

What activities bring you joy?

How often do you do them?

Wouldn't it be wonderful to be able to say that everything you do brings you joy?

How often do you feel joy?

If you want to attract the money, health and relationships you desire then you need to cultivate a life of joy.

You already know how to write down what you appreciate and I hope you are doing it every day. If you want to enhance this appreciation and it's affects, tap while you speak your appreciation out loud.

Activity 27

If you haven't already done so start writing down, on a daily basis, 10 things you feel appreciation toward. As I've said before, they can be very simple things or very big things. Some days you might only have small things and that's ok.

Take each of the 10 things and say: "I appreciate (fill in the blank with your appreciation)" as you tap on each of the tapping points in turn. One item per tapping point. Do 10 rounds of tapping on the 10 items.

For Example:

Eyebrow point: I really appreciate it when my husband makes me coffee in the morning.

Side of the Eye: I really appreciate the way my cat cuddles up beside me and purrs.

Under the Eye: I appreciate finding that parking space this morning.

Under the Nose: I appreciate the way the clear ocean reflects the blue sky.

Above the Chin: I appreciate the sound of the trees rustling in the wind.

Collarbone: I appreciate how we were able to get that drain unblocked so easily.

Under the Arm: I appreciate that I now know how to tap so that I can change my life and begin to attract the things I want into my life.

Repeat 10 times every day.

If you still find some negative emotions or thoughts interrupting your day then take time out to tap through the negative emotions. Once you've finished tapping through them do the activity above making sure to focus on what you appreciate.

The goal is to release the limiting thoughts and feelings and replace them with helpful thoughts so that you can raise your level of joy and feel it more frequently.

The Art of Receiving

We've already talked about the need to forget about how the manifestation of your desire is going to happen. You can certainly mentally entertain all of the novel ways it can happen but don't get hung up on them being the "only" way.

Part of the art of receiving is standing back and letting the universe get on with bringing to you what you have intended. This means that you also need to be open to receiving what it is that you want.

So that means that you need to know what it is that you want. You need to feel worthy of it in order to allow yourself to receive it. You then need to trust the universe to deliver it to you while you step out of the way and get on with life.

Being open to receiving is letting go of your desire and allowing yourself to accept it when it comes. So, go back and look at your story and really ask yourself if you are open to receiving it.

How Other People Affect Your Magnetism

Getting what you want will change your life.

Are you ready for that change?

Are the people around you ready for that change?

Which people around you will be happy for you when you achieve your desire?

Which people around you will not be very happy for you when you achieve your desire?

Sometimes our blocks can be about other people. We may feel that they will be angry, fearful or just don't want the change to occur for their own reasons. If you know this about your significant others, then your subconscious mind will construct blocks to your progress.

This is where you need to make a decision about what you really want to do. What is more important to you. You can stay as you are or you can move forward.

Once you make the choice the other people in your

life will either come around to your new way of being, even if they were afraid at first, or they will gravitate away from you.

As you make changes to yourself you will find that different people will come into your life and other people will leave. That's normal. We attract people based on our own beliefs about ourselves.

If we doubt ourselves, we will surround ourselves with people who will support that doubt in some way. Even if they seem supportive and encouraging, they may still influence you in subtle ways.

Once you begin to feel better about yourself in the present moment, you'll start to see how other people are reacting to you. If you are feeling not good enough, unworthy or guilty go back through the previous activities that address those feelings and tap on them.

Change the phrasing to suit the details of what you are feeling now. Tapping scripts are only a guideline. You can never say anything wrong.

The best tapping comes from simply expressing how you feel and what you are thinking until those feelings start to shift in some way. Sometimes, it may take a number of days of tapping on the same issue before you feel the shift.

The key is to persevere with it until you feel better.

PART FIVE

LIVING FROM YOUR POWER

In this final section you're going to focus on the steps you need to take in order for you to achieve the best results with this work. These steps are:

Know what you want.

Identify how you feel about it.

Release any blocks

Focusing your intention

Getting out of the way and open to receiving.

You will also find some fun and useful tools that you can use to help you focus on your intention. The more fun you have when you are focusing your intent the more likely you will achieve the kind of result you are looking for.

I will also show you some fun ways to build and harness your magnetism. Magnetism is an art and like any art you have to practise it to be good at it.

You can use law of attraction every day. The more you

use it the better you will get at it. Regular practise builds confidence because you'll see it working every day.

Once you start seeing the results, you'll know that you're really on to something magical. This of course makes your life magical. Imagine feeling like your life is blessed every day!

Does that sound good to you?

The more creative you can be with manifesting the more fun you will have. We are creative beings after all. There are so many creative techniques that you can use to help motivate you and enliven your intention so that you can create more powerfully.

Let's begin creating that life you want so much!

CHAPTER ELEVEN

Creating Your Life

You now have a powerful tool that you can use to not only remove your blocks to manifesting but also to enhance your power to magnetise. In this chapter you're going to proceed step by step through the manifestation process.

When you follow this process, you can't go wrong with manifesting. But you MUST follow it 100% if you want the absolute best results.

Step One – Know What You Want

So, what do you want?

Your desire should be as specific as you can make it. It could be along the lines of a new relationship, a new car, a better job, solving a particular problem or finding your life purpose.

We've covered this in previous chapters. You can easily find out what you do want by knowing what you don't want. I've suggested before that you write down what it is that you don't want and then write down what you do want beside it.

This sounds easy enough but I want to mention that

it is quite common for people to not know what they really want. We've gone through our whole lives being told what we should want and what we shouldn't want that sometimes we just don't know.

We often knew what we wanted as children but so often these dreams and ambitions are stifled and discouraged. Many of us were even punished for expressing what we wanted. This can make knowing what we want very difficult.

Sometimes it's been buried so deep within ourselves that we just can't access it. There might even be shame and guilt associated with what we want. This can certainly suppress it.

This is the point where we need to be honest with ourselves. So, in step one, it's about discovering and honouring what it is we want to achieve in our life at the present time.

These achievements can be on a material level, relationship level or a deeper life purpose level. Creating is creating. There is no need to become hung up on being torn between spiritual and materiel goals. When we're on this planet we need both.

Sometimes, the material goals are needed to support a deeper purpose. Feel free to use your magnetic ability to attract what you need on all levels. Be brave and dare to want. Dare to explore what you want.

If you feel any shame or guilt over what you want, don't worry about that now. You'll get to deal with all of the limiting feelings and beliefs in Step 2 and 3.

Let's look at some of the techniques you can use to find out what it is that you want.

List what you don't want and then list what you

would like instead next to each item.

Visualise your desire or perfect situation. Watch yourself living your desire. Spend about 5 to 10 minutes doing this. This is your opportunity to live your desire on the mental level so really go for it.

Act out who you are in this desired situation. You might want to lock yourself away from other people to do this or they might think you've gone crazy. Acting out is great if you aren't a visual person. Just pretend you're an actor rehearsing a role because in effect that's what you are doing.

Record yourself telling a story about your perfect day. Make sure you mention who is there, where you are and what is around you.

You can use these ideas later in step 4 when you learn how to enhance your magnetism and really boost your ability to succeed.

Step Two – Identify How You Feel

Once you've spent some time imagining yourself in the desired situation, notice how you feel about it. You can do this in the following ways:

Write your feelings next to what you want on your list.

Write your feelings down as you go through your vision.

Speak your feelings out loud into a recording device as you are telling the story to yourself.

Notice how your body feels as you act out your story.

Identifying your feelings is really important. It's important because not being aware of your negative feelings is the reason why your manifestation hasn't been working for you so far.

Please don't skip this part. Don't skip any part but particularly this part. This work has to be done and the feelings confronted if you REALLY want to see the changes in your life.

Nothing will change for you if you don't confront the icky stuff. They are just feelings after all and now you know how to tap you can tap away those feelings in a relatively short space of time.

So be thorough with this 2nd step.

Step 3 – Release the Limiting Beliefs and Feelings

Remember that your emotions are your guidance system. They let you know when you're not aligned with your true desire. From your emotions you can find the thoughts that are at the root cause of those uncomfortable and often distressing feelings.

Of course, you already know how to release those negative thoughts and feelings through tapping. Let's just summarise the steps:

Rate how strong your feeling is on the 0 to 10 scale with 10 being strong and 0 being nothing at all.

Take one feeling at a time and use that in your set up statement in relation to your desire. For example:

Even though I feel discouraged when I think about my desire to own my own business, I deeply and completely love, honour and accept myself.

Now you're ready to make up your set-up statement. You can either use ones from the scripts in this book or you can simply use your own. The simplest way to do this is to identify the emotion and then use it for each point. For example:

Eyebrow point: This feeling of discouragement.

Side of the Eye: I feel so discouraged

Under the Eye: I feel so discouraged when I think about owning my own business.

Under the Nose: I feel so discouraged.

Above the Chin: All of this discouragement.

Collarbone: So much discouragement when I think about owning my own business.

Under the Arm: I just feel so discouraged.

As you do about 4 or 5 rounds of tapping you will find that other thoughts and ideas will come up for you. Verbalise those thoughts and ideas as you tap. Simply substitute them for the feeling.

Alternatively, you can have a conversation with yourself while you are tapping on the points. Talk about how you feel and verbalise the limiting thoughts behind them. Keep tapping on these until the emotional volume decreases.

It's important that you tap until the feelings are down to a 1 or 0. Once your feelings are at about a 4 you should then introduce some alternative ways to think using "What if" statements. For example:

What if I can run a successful business on my own?

What if I can become confident around people?

Adding "what if" statements challenges your cognitive pattern. However, only start to do this once you're a 4 or less on the 0 to 10 scale. There's no point doing it beforehand as your subconscious mind won't even consider it.

Step 4 – Focusing Your Intent

This is where you get to be creative with your desire. There are as many ways to enhance your intent as there are people so use your creativity and find fun ways for focusing your intent.

Basically, you have to do some time travelling and imagine your desire as if it has already happened. This should be easier once you've tapped on the blocks.

You need to experience how your desire feels NOW as if it HAS happened. Feel how happy you feel, the more intense the feeling the better.

Now you'll know if your tapping has wiped out all of the limiting beliefs or not because if you don't feel joy then you still have work to do.

If you can't really FEEL joy and happiness go back and either review your desire (maybe you don't want it anymore) or find the limiting beliefs and do some more tapping.

Totally fill your mind with the details of what's happening in your future vision. Concentrate on the feeling of joy and exhilaration. Build those feelings so that they are as strong as you can make them.

I'm going to show you some ways that you can enhance the feelings and mental associations with your desire. You have no limits here but you can start with the suggestions below. It can be as simple or as creative and artistic as you like.

When you use these techniques don't stop until you feel like what you want has already happened. Remember when you focus on something you are focusing on a possible reality.

Feel how right it is that you have what you want. Keep doing the visualisation and other methods until you feel like you have what it is that you want. You might need to do multiple sessions until you achieve this but it's worth spending the time on.

It's important to use as many senses as you can when focusing on your intention because they all work together on your subconscious mind. So find ways that you can use vision, sound, smell, taste and touch to enhance your feelings of happiness and accomplishment.

The more your senses elevate your feelings the more your subconscious mind will become convinced that what you're imagining is really happening. This will reinforce the subconscious belief that you have it already and the universe with reflect it back to you.

To enhance your associations and happy feelings about your desire try the following:

Option One

You're going to make a mini vision board, however, instead of putting it up where you can see it every day, you're going to work in a more traditional magical way.

Use separate boards for each thing you want. For example, create a board for a relationship, a board for money, a board for travel. Don't do one big board for everything you want.

Use paper for this instead of cardboard. Cut out pictures and even text from the magazines that correspond to your desire and stick them onto the paper.

As you create your vision board just imagine yourself in the image as if you are looking at a photograph of yourself in that image.

Try to imagine what scents you might be smelling in that image and the sounds you maybe hearing as well. This will help you feel more motivated and will trick your subconscious mind into believing that it is really happening.

You can decorate it in any way you like.

Add some attraction-based herbs to your board, such as:

Rose petals for love and romance

Cinnamon for money

Ground ginger for success

Bless your board by stating what it is intended to do for you and then fold it in half toward you. I'll tell you what to do with it soon.

Option Two

Buy a coloured piece of paper that you feel corresponds with your desire and write down what you want in one sentence. Really try to get the essence of what you want in the one sentence.

Below are some traditional colours and their associations:

Red – love and passion, relationships

Pink – friendships

Green – money and growth

Yellow – ideas and electronic finance

Blue – healing and health, peace

Purple – life purpose

You can use the colour scale with all kinds of things, from pens to candles.

Light a coloured candle using the table above or use your own associations and verbalise your desire out loud while you gaze at the flame.

Option Three

Use tapping to enhance your emotional feelings. Alternate between saying I want and I have.

Eyebrow point: *I want a loving relationship.*
Side of the Eye: *I have a loving relationship.*
Under the Eye: *I want a loving relationship.*
Under the Nose: *I have a loving relationship.*
Above the Chin: *I want a loving relationship.*
Collarbone: *I have a loving relationship.*
Under the Arm: *I want a loving relationship.*

Repeat the tapping sequence as many times as it takes until you feel like it has already happened.

Option Four

Use aromatherapy to enhance your feelings. Simply burn some oil in a burner that correspond with your desire and close your eyes and imagine it all happening.

Try the associations below:

Rose oil – love and romance,

Patchouli oil – money and prosperity

Find a piece of music that you really like that makes you feel fantastic, enlivened and that you can associate with the YOU in your story. Play it as you visualise your desire. You can even dance the joy if dancing is your thing.

These are just some suggestions for ways that you can incorporate sight, smell, sound and touch into your intention. Remember the more senses that are involved the more real it becomes to the subconscious mind.

The ideas are only as limited as your creativity. Enjoy the process and you'll get far greater results then you've ever achieved before.

Step Five – Getting Out of The Way and Open to Receiving

How do you get out of the way?

Well first you need to surrender. That's right! You need to trust that what you desire has already happened and will come into physical manifestation at the right time and place.

There are ways that you can symbolically do this. The subconscious mind loves symbols. Try some symbolic activities that correspond to letting go and trusting that the universe is going to bring it all to you. This will help convince your subconscious mind that it's happened.

Sensory activities are merely tools to communicate to the subconscious mind that what you imagined has happened and that you are no longer desperate or attached to the result.

Remember the subconscious mind can't differentiate between what is imagined and what is real. So use this to your advantage!

Some of the ideas below may seem silly and a bit like

you're living in a magical fairytale but once again, the subconscious mind speaks in symbols so use it all to your advantage. Be as creative as you can be.

So, see below for ways that you can get out of the way and surrender to the universe.

Option One

If you've used the vision board method do the following:

Open yourself to receiving by symbolically giving it up to the Universe using any of the following methods:

Burn the board in a safe fireplace

Bury it in your garden (make sure it's buried on your property)

Give it to a river or the ocean (not so environmentally friendly so make sure you haven't used hazardous materials)

Put it away in a manifestation box.

Now, I know that this contradicts the usual idea that you should put it somewhere where you will see it often. Well, surrendering doesn't work that way.

By ceremoniously give up your vision board you're allowing yourself to forget about it which is exactly what you need to do to make it all happen.

You're also sending your request out into the world of manifestation.

So, create your board and then surrender it to the universe.

Option Two

If you've written your intention on coloured paper burn the paper or throw it into a living body of water. But, do this only after you've gotten to the point where you are sure that it has happened and you are at the height of your joy.

Once again, it's about symbolically surrendering to the universe. It's all about trust and letting go of the NEED for the desire to happen. You're trying to send a message to the subconscious mind that you are letting go.

If you're using a coloured candle, put it somewhere safe, like the bathtub or shower and allow it to burn down. If you can't let it burn safely then snuff it out and light it again the next day. Keep doing this until it does burn all the way down.

Throw any remaining materials into a living body of water or bury it in your garden.

Option Three

When you use tapping to enhance your intention. Simply do a round of tapping where you say:

I let go and trust that this has occurred for my greater good.

If you've used music, simply replay the music until you are convinced that your desire has happened and then let the music finish. When the music finishes just say:

I let go and trust that this has occurred for my greater good.

Now that you have let go and surrendered, immediately take you mind off your desire and do something else. Distract yourself. Deliberately focus on something else.

If you start to think of your desire at all, just tell yourself that it's happened and then think of something else.

Go about your day feeling as if your desire has happened. This will further convince your subconscious mind that you are living the reality you want to live and it will attract more of the same.

CHAPTER TWELVE

Living A Life by Design

Creating Change

Creating the life you want does take work. There are no simple formulas. If it was as easy as it's often made out then everyone would be doing it. The truth is that most people aren't prepared to do the real work to make it happen.

In order to create the change, we want to see around us we have to create change inside of us. It's our inner world that is being mirrored back to us by the universe.

Manifestation is all about creating change from the inside. We must create change via our subconscious mind and our thinking habits before we will see results in the outer world.

Creating change takes courage. Becoming more magnetic takes discipline and practise. Most people aren't courageous enough to be able to do this.

So, if you're serious about choosing a life by design instead of a life of reaction then you will implement the strategies in this book. You'll work at clearing out those inner blocks that prevent you from being the person you want to be. This will bring you closer to the life you want.

Only You Can Change You

It's true, you are the only one who can manifest what you want. You are the only one who can change you. Increasing your magnetism requires you to commit to yourself.

There are certain things you will need to do on a daily basis that will help you become a powerful magnet to what you want, but you have to be prepared to make that commitment to you.

We call it turning up for yourself. You must turn up for yourself before you can turn up for anyone else. You must put the time and energy into reprogramming your thinking and bravely take on new beliefs and behaviours.

This means taking time out every day to focus on bringing yourself into a more positive and receptive state of being. There are a number of ways that you can do this.

One way to make your intention clearer and stronger for you is to write yourself a contract. It might go something like the following:

I (your name) commit to myself and my desire to lead a life by design by committing to _____, _____ and _____ on a daily basis. I acknowledge that this is a commitment to me which is absolutely necessary in order for me to live the life I want.

Fill in the blank with whatever activities you feel will bring you closer to living your life the way you want. For example, you might include tapping, meditation, creative visualisation or prayer.

Self-Care

If you want a better life, a life that is one of thriving instead of just surviving then you have to understand the concept of self-care. The problem is that this may sound selfish to some people.

If you haven't already done so you might want to go back to the section on tapping on selfishness and guilt. Often when we consider committing to something for ourselves, we can be hit with a huge guilt trip.

We are programmed to give and give and give, especially if we see ourselves as spiritual. Everyone else is supposed to come first. I'm not proposing narcissism here but in order to have what you want you do need to be selfish to some degree. This selfishness is mostly in regard to your time and energy.

It's true that in order to love others you must love yourself first and in order to help others you have to help yourself first. Constant giving is draining and like it or not it most often causes feelings of resentment and frustration.

Learning to say no to people is the first step to taking back your power and conserving your energy. Sure, some people will call you selfish but you must ask the question: Who is being selfish? In most cases it's you and them. So, whose selfishness is going to win, yours or theirs?

You have to be the judge of how you delegate your time but in order to have what you want you must learn to be a little more selfish with your time so that you have the mental and emotional energy to pursue your goals.

Manifesting what you want and designing your life is a skill and like all skills you must practise. The more you practise the more results you'll see and the more results you see the more confident you'll become.

It follows that the more confident you become the better you'll be able to manifest. So now that I've said that, let's look at some of the ways that you can show up for you and practise the life of a magical creator.

Make A Time for You

Make a time everyday where you take some time out for you. I'm going to list some activities which I recommend that you do most days if not every day. You can alternate between some activities if you're challenged for time.

However, even being challenged for time is something we manifest. If you need more time then work on manifesting more time first. The best times to do this work are just as you wake up in the morning and before you go to bed at night, but anytime is sufficient. You can even break these activities up into small portions throughout the day.

Meditation

There are many forms of meditation and different forms work better for different people. The type of meditation that I recommend is a simple mindfulness meditation whereby you just concentrate on your breath in and out for at least 15 minutes.

BUT if you're not used to meditating start out by

doing only 3 minutes and build up to 15. You'll only get frustrated if you try to sit there for 15 minutes while your mind races from thought to thought.

It's natural for your thoughts to wander during meditation. The important thing is to simply bring your focus back to your breathing. Don't judge yourself for letting your thoughts wander because they will.

Keep bringing the mind home to the breath.

There are a couple of things that you can add to this process depending on whether you're visually, auditory or kinaesthetically orientated.

If you're visual, light a candle and concentrate on the flame while focusing on your breathing.

If you're auditory, you can focus on the sounds around you without becoming distracted by them. It's even better if you can meditate near the ocean, a waterfall or somewhere where there are natural sounds. Simply listen to the sound while gently focusing on your breathing.

If you are a body person or kinaesthetic then focus on being in your body while you meditate. Feel the floor or cushion under your backside and sense your body in space and the space around your body. Do this while also focusing on your breathing.

These extra sensory stimulants help the mind focus. It's easier to meditate if you have something to focus upon.

Make sure that you are physically comfortable while meditating. You can sit on the floor with your legs crossed and your back straight or if that's not comfortable or practical sit in a chair with you back supported in an upright and aligned position.

The goal with this kind of meditation is to quiet the mind and relax the body. You will find that this will help increase your ability to concentrate which will make it easier to focus on your intentions for a longer period of time.

Create A Tapping Journal

Journaling is a great way to keep track of your progress in many ways. Keeping a journal that's dedicated to your tapping as well as your manifesting will help you see your progress with both.

Record what you're feeling or thinking in your journal and rate the feeling on the 0 to 10 scale. As you tap you will find that memories or other thoughts will often come into your awareness. When this happens, write these down.

It's not possible to tap on everything at the same time. The way around this is to write down any new ideas and thoughts so that you can come back to them later.

Memories are really important too. It's common to have memories come up for you when you're tapping. These memories may be related to what you're tapping on or they may seem unrelated. Write them all down.

If a memory has come up for you while you're tapping then it will be relevant to what you're tapping on. Otherwise, it wouldn't come up. Feel free to tap on the memory if it's not too traumatic. We haven't dealt with memories in the book so go easy on yourself here.

As I've said in the very beginning it's important that you work with what is safe for you. If any traumatic events come up and you are having trouble working through them then please seek the help of a qualified therapist or EFT practitioner.

Try to keep tapping on the same theme until it's down to a 1 or a 0. You can then move on to something else afterwards.

This process is much like peeling the layers of an onion. There are often many layers to our programming and it can take some time to peel them all away.

Track Your Wins

Keeping track of your manifestation goals and accomplishments is a great way to build confidence in your ability to manifest. Each time you focus on what you want and it comes to you, write it down.

As you write down your wins, always thank the universe for bringing it to you because that will increase your feeling of appreciation.

Sometimes it takes a while before you see results. Some things may be too way outside of your sphere of availability at this time. That doesn't mean that events, people and situations aren't coming into alignment. It may take some time for it all to synchronise.

When you record your desire always rate how you feel about it coming true for you. Rate how much you believe it can happen on the 0 to 10 scale. 10 is for the strong feeling that it will definitely happen and 0 is if you feel that it just can't happen.

Once you've rated your belief then start tapping on the reasons why you think that it can't happen. Always remember that you aren't the one who makes things happen. You don't know the bigger picture and can't see all of the possibilities and processes that have to align before it can happen.

So even if you can't figure out how it's going to happen, that's not an excuse to believe it can't happen. So, tap it out.

Daily Manifesting

Just as a musician must practise their instrument on a daily basis, so you too will benefit from practising your manifesting daily as well.

Many people use their intentions to find parking spaces. I do this regularly with great success. I've also used it find good restaurants and household items that are difficult to come by.

Basically, you can use the law of attraction all of the time. You do unconsciously anyway so why not do it regularly on a conscious level.

When you wake up in the morning set an intention for how you want your day to go. New year's resolutions are a form of intention. Unfortunately, they aren't always approached with the necessary mental discipline to see them to fruition.

Now you know how to manifest and remove all of the blocks, you can set intentions on a yearly, monthly, weekly and daily basis.

Why not try to set an intention that you will receive $200 in the near future. Once you achieve that increase it to $500. Keep increasing the amount and see what happens.

I once set myself the goal of seeing a hippopotamus. I set the goal to include photos and pictures as well as the real thing. I don't live anywhere near a zoo and I don't come across hippos at all even on face book. So, my chances of seeing a real hippo or a photo of one were pretty slim.

I set myself the goal of seeing one within two days. Toward the end of the second day I was looking at a calendar and turned the page over to the next month, and there was a picture of 3 hippos.

I've done the same thing with money and have often been surprised at where it manifests from. Sometimes I'll receive some money that someone may owe me. Other times I might receive a gift or I might win a voucher. The universe always seems to find a way to get it to me.

So have fun with this and set yourself little goals at first and then raise them higher and higher. We're here to create.

Thought Watching

It's good to get into the habit of regularly taking a mental step back and just focus on what you are thinking in the moment. Especially if you are feeling an uncomfortable emotion or stress.

You can write your thoughts down in your tapping journal and tap on them when it's convenient. Doing this will make you more aware of what yoy're thinking and how your thoughts dictate how you feel.

This is important if you are wanting to attract more of what you want into your life. It's a must if you want a life of joy and prosperity. Remember, your thoughts reflect your beliefs and your beliefs come from your experiences and programming. They directly affect what you manifest on a subconscious level.

People Watching

I'm not proposing that you become judgemental toward other people here. People watching is about observing other people so that you can learn from them.

People give away a lot about themselves by the way they dress, walk, speak, and carry themselves. You can guess at times what kind of things a person manifests into their life simply by how a person presents themselves.

As your life changes for the better you will notice new people coming into your life and other people leaving it. Take notice of the differences between people and what they are all manifesting in their lives.

This can help you look at yourself so you can better use the technique of acting "as if" your desire and lifestyle have already occurred.

If you know of someone who has what you want then study them. Look at how they walk, talk and carry themselves. Like an actor, take on their characteristics just as an exercise and see how you feel. See if it changes anything.

It should change the way you feel. Changing your body posture will influence your emotions because emotions are expressed through your body. Try it and see.

All of the techniques above allow you to become more conscious of yourself on a daily basis. You need to become more conscious of yourself so that you can obtain mastery over yourself and your life.

You are the only one who can manifest what you want.

It's up to you to use every tool you can to develop self-awareness and self-discipline. You need these in order to design your life the way you want it. Otherwise, you will just be swept about life like a jellyfish is swept around by the ocean.

People try to make out that manifesting the life you want is easy. Well, it is and it isn't. The hardest part is in the surrendering. It's the trust in the universe and trust in ourselves that determines how easy or difficult it is to consciously and deliberately manifest what we want.

If you implement all of the strategies in this book you should be well on the way to creating the life you want. It takes courage to make change and I congratulate you on being one of the few people on the planet who are willing to make such changes.

CONCLUSION

I hope you've enjoyed the process of becoming a magnetic creator. I know that some of it hasn't been easy. Digging down deeply into the subconscious mind isn't always fun. I congratulate you on taking the time out for yourself and doing the tapping activities.

Being a powerful magnet to what you want does demand that you know yourself. That means getting to know you, taking risks and learning to trust yourself.

Learning the art of manifestation is a journey into personal development. So many people just think that law of attraction is a simple means of thinking of something you want and manifesting it. You probably know by now that it's not that simple.

This process is as much a personal understanding process as it is a method of making your life more materially comfortable.

So, in this book you have learned how the law of attraction works and how your mind works. You've learned how important your subconscious programs are and how to change them as well.

You've also learned a very powerful technique called EFT that can help you find your limiting programs and change them. Not only that, EFT can be used to help you manifest what you want. How good is that!

You've even discovered your hidden motives and know how to focus on feeling good in the present moment. Now you can live your dream story in the present which will help you manifest more of what you do want into your future.

Now that you know the five-step process to designing the life you want you can make all of the adjustments necessary to make it all happen. You can utilise the extra tools and techniques that I've given you to help you feel more excited and powerful while you are concentrating on what you want.

Finally, now you know how you can get out of the way of the universe and let it deliver the results to you. Remember, you aren't the actual creator, the universe is.

ABOUT THE AUTHOR

Sandra Inman's interest in EFT Tapping was sparked by a series of anxiety attacks in 2014. Having struggled with low self-esteem and social anxiety as a child, Sandra was no stranger to how limiting life can be when we believe we are unworthy, unlovable and undeserving.

She has been a practising EFT Tapping practitioner since 2015 and now helps people all over the world recover their true selves using EFT, Hypnotherapy, Shamanic practices and various other modalities.

Her interest in the law of attraction stems from a 30-year Wiccan practice. Sandra says, "When I first heard about the law of attraction, I was so excited to see magic making a comeback". Sandra utilises what she has learned about magic from her Wiccan practice and blends this with the law of attraction principles to create a manifestation process that is both transformative and empowering.

Book a FREE Clarity Session with Sandra to discover you biggest blocks to manifestation and what steps you can take to break free and create the life you want to live.

https://mysterywitchschool.coachesconsole.com/calendar/

Email:
sandra@mysterywitchschool.com

YouTube:
https://www.youtube.com/c/SandraInmanTapping
https://www.youtube.com/c/MysticalWitchSchool

Website:
https://mysterywitchschool.coachesconsole.com/

BIBLIOGRAPHY

Barden, Gregg, Resilience From The Heart: The power To Thrive In Lifes's Extremems. Australia: Hay House, INC. 2015

Byrne, Rhonda, The Secret. New York: Atria Books. 2006

Dispenza, Joe, Breaking the Habit of Being Yourself. Australia: Hay House, INC. 2015

Doidge, Norman, MD. The Brain That Changes Itself. Australia: Scribe Publications Pty ltd. 2010

Hicks, Esther and Jerry, The Law of attraction: Essential Collection. Australia: Hay House, INC. 2013

Hoobyar, Tom & Dotz, Tom & Sanders, Susan, NLP The Essential Guide To Neuo-Linguistic Programming. NY: Harper Collins, 2013

Lipton, Bruce H, Ph.D. The Biology of Belief: Unleashing the Power of Consciousness, Matter and Miracles. Australia: Hay House, INC.2014

Lynch, Margaret, Tapping into Wealth. USA: Penguin, 2013

Solomon, Kathilyn, Tapping into Wellness: Using EFT to Clear Emotional & PhysicalPain & Illness. USA: Llewellyn Worldwise Ltd, 2015

Printed in Dunstable, United Kingdom